CAREERS IN BANKING AND FINANCE

By
PATRICIA HADDOCK

The Rosen Publishing Group, Inc.
NEW YORK

Published in 1990, 1998 by The Rosen Publishing Group, Inc.
29 East 21st Street, New York, NY 10010

Revised Edition 1998

Library of Congress Cataloging-in-Publication Data

Haddock, Patricia
  Careers in banking and finance/by Patricia Haddock.
    p. cm.
  Includes bibliographical references.
  Summary: Describes the various jobs available in banking and finance and the education and training required.
  ISBN 0-8239-2533-1
  1. Banks and banking—Vocational guidance—United States—Juvenile literature. 2. Financial services industry—Vocational guidance—United States—Juvenile literature. [1. Banks and banking—Vocational guidance. 2. Financial services industry—Vocational guidance. 3. Vocational guidance.] I. Title.
HG1609.H33   1989
332.1'023'73—dc20   89-37693
                                                                CIP
                                                                AC

Manufactured in the United States of America

Acknowledgments

I want to say "Thanks" to several people who took time to help make this book more interesting:

Public relations rep Tara Ranels Little at the American Bankers Association, who coordinated the interviews and photos that I needed from her home, where she was awaiting the birth of her baby.

John Scully at the Pacific Stock Exchange, who gathered together busy traders for me to talk to.

George Frankenstein, who juggled his calendar to do a last-minute interview.

Editor and friend Heidi Garfield, who gave me access to her file of banking photos.

Professional photographers Mike Bloomensaadt, who gave me three of his best photos for the cost of the prints, and Lewis Stewart, who provided two badly needed shots at the last minute.

And to Ruth Rosen, who has more patience than most.

Many thanks and much appreciation!

About the Author

Patricia Haddock owns a communications consulting business in San Francisco. She has written and produced a wide range of corporate communications, including brochures, newsletters, and speeches. Her clients include major banks, insurance companies, and entrepreneurs.

In addition to corporate communications, Ms. Haddock has sold five books and more than 200 articles to more than 150 magazines, including *Delta Sky*, *Seventeen*, *Woman's Day*, and *Sylvia Porter's Personal Finance*. She specializes in business, self-help, and creativity subjects and also teaches and lectures on writing, creativity, and public speaking.

Before becoming a full-time consultant, Ms. Haddock worked as a communications officer and manager for a major California bank. She is listed in *Who's Who in the West* and *Author's and Writer's Who's Who*. She is a member of the American Society of Journalists and Authors, the Authors Guild, the Society of Children's Book Writers and Illustrators, and the Associated Business Writers of America.

Contents

Introduction   1

1. Banking: Changes and Challenges   4
2. Finance: The World of Wall Street   19
3. Choosing the Right Job in Banking
   and Finance   26

   Accountant and Auditor   26
   Bank Teller   29
   Bookkeeper and Accounting Clerk   34
   Broker   35
   Clerical Supervisor and Manager   42
   Commercial Banker   43
   Commodity Trader   47
   Computer Operator   49
   Data Entry Keyer   51
   Economist   52
   File Clerk   53
   Financial Manager   55
   Financial Planner   57
   Human Resources   64
   Institutional Broker   65
   Investment Banker   67
   Lawyer   73
   Marketing   75
   Research Analyst   76
   Secretary   78
   Trader   79
   Trust Officer   85
   Typist and Word Processor   86

4. Insider Information 87
5. Getting the Job You Want 90

Glossary 106
Appendix 118
For Further Reading 121
Index 123

Introduction

Imagine turning on your computer and being able to pay your bills, find out your checking account balance, or apply for a loan. Imagine buying and selling stocks online while eating breakfast, or exchanging American dollars for foreign currency without ever leaving home. Imagine buying everything from stamps to movie tickets at the nearest ATM—but only after having your eye scanned by a laser that can identify you by the pattern of blood vessels in your retina.

It may sound like science fiction, but it's not. Chances are that your own local bank offers most, if not all, of these services now. New technologies like these are changing the way financial companies do business. Customers are suddenly able to perform many of the functions that bank tellers and brokers once did. This has changed many jobs in the field of banking and finance.

Some people predict that we are in the midst of a revolution in financial services. They say that banks in the twenty-first century will look quite different—and perform different functions—than banks today. In part this is due to the availability of advanced technology, and in part because banks and brokerages now offer similar services.

Until recently, banks and brokerages were different types of businesses. Each offered unique services and products. Banks offered checking and savings accounts and made loans, while brokerages sold stocks and bonds. A person worked in banking or in a brokerage and rarely moved from one to the other. The two worlds were highly regulated by federal and state laws, and there was not much competition between banking and finance.

Then, in the early 1980s, the government began to remove many of the regulations that had previously separated banking and finance. With deregulation came competition. Suddenly banks and brokerages were competing for the same customers and offering similar products and services. Large banks began to buy smaller banks. Companies began to pour money into new technology in order to keep up with the competition and position themselves on the cutting edge of the financial world. What was once a rather staid profession became a high-powered and highly competitive industry.

Deregulation has also opened the door to opportunity. Once careers in banking and finance followed pretty straight lines. That is no longer true. Today banking and finance are not really two different worlds. Some jobs are still unique to one; for instance, brokerage houses don't have tellers and banks don't have retail brokers. But in most areas, banks and financial services companies offer the same services and products. Careers in one are the same as careers in the other, or very similar. For instance, both industries need research analysts, so those skills can be transferred from a bank to a brokerage and vice versa. The opportunity for crossover in the two fields increases the number of jobs available for qualified people.

The jobs in this book are described in broad terms. Although they are common jobs in banking and finance, their duties, their importance within a company, and the career opportunities they offer vary from corporation to corporation.

This book gives you broad ideas about the jobs available. You must talk to different companies to determine where your personality will fit best, how the jobs you are interested in are staffed, how employees are trained, and how far and where you can go with the company. The chapter titled "Choosing the Right Job in Banking and Finance" and the Appendix will help you find that out.

1

Banking: Changes and Challenges

"If you define success as tackling exciting challenges and dealing with change, as well as making a real difference to the economic and social welfare of the communities in which you live and work, then banking is a pretty good career to consider."

Robert N. Beck
Executive Vice President
Bank of America

In the past, being a banker meant processing savings and checking deposits and withdrawals from customers' accounts, lending money to businesses and individuals, and making sure all the money balanced at the end of the day. Sometimes you opened a safe deposit box for someone.

People believed that bankers ran their businesses according to the Rule of 3–6–3: Pay 3 percent on deposits; charge 6 percent on loans; get to the golf course by 3:00 p.m.

No one believes that anymore. Banking has changed, and changed drastically.

Banking today is one of the most competitive and exciting industries in the world. Bank of America and Chase compete not only with all other banks, but with nonbank companies such as Merrill Lynch and Fidelity Investments.

Once upon a time banks could count on keeping customers forever. They can no longer do that. Customer loyalty to one bank is largely a thing of the past. Customers look for the best return on their money, convenience, and a variety of products that meet their financial needs.

Unsteady interest rates, demanding customers, deregulation of the banking industry, and competition from not only banks but also other financial and nonfinancial industries have all contributed to the changing world of banking. To survive and thrive, banks must meet their competition head-on. And that means that opportunities exist for sharp, eager, ambitious young people who want to participate in the world of money and finance.

A Short History of Banking

Banks and bankers have been around for thousands of years, but modern banking dates only from the sixteenth century, when Italian bankers conducted their business from benches. The word "bank" comes from the Italian word for bench: *banca.*

In England goldsmiths took on the role of bankers. Wealthy people, usually merchants, stored their gold and silver in a goldsmith's vault. The goldsmith, in turn, gave the owners receipts for the gold, and the merchants used their receipts to get credit. The receipts proved that they could pay for the merchandise they ordered.

The goldsmiths soon discovered that they could lend the gold and silver they stored for the merchants and charge interest to the people who borrowed it. They could also attract more merchants to deposit gold and silver with them by paying interest. So the English goldsmiths became bankers.

Early in America's history banks often issued their own money. If you lived on a farm near Lincoln, Nebraska, you paid your bills with money issued by your local Lincoln bank. People living in New Orleans used money issued by a New Orleans bank. Almost as many currencies were in circulation as there were banks. It was very confusing, especially if you traveled. It was also dangerous.

If one of the banks failed, depositors lost the money they had on deposit with the bank. All the money the bank had issued was also lost. It was totally worthless!

The U.S. government decided that something had to be done to safeguard the value of money, and Congress passed the National Bank Acts of 1863 and 1864 to create a trustworthy paper currency. The worth of the money depended on the federal government, not individual banks.

Early banks offered little in the way of careers. They were much smaller than today's banks and usually had only two employees: the president and a clerk. The president acted as cashier, making loans and running the business. The clerk acted as teller and bookkeeper. Most of the transactions they handled were cash, but checks became popular after the Civil War. Soon after that banks started making real estate and personal loans.

Then in 1929 the stock market crashed. Many banks suffered overwhelming losses from which they could not recover. Banks closed, unable to give people back the money they had on deposit.

Some people lost their entire life savings in one day. Many of the bank failures were caused because bankers had used bank money to make various investments in the stock market. Some of those investments were very risky. When the market crashed, the banks failed.

In order to prevent a recurrence of this kind of financial catastrophe, Congress decided to separate

The lines separating banking and brokerage are blurring. An electronic Dow-Jones ticker tape on a Charles Schwab board dominates one wall of the lobby of Bank of America's main office (courtesy Matrix).

commercial banks, which take deposits, from investment banks, which underwrite corporate securities. That means that the bank buys an issue of bonds or stock from a company and then sells the securities to investors. Commercial banks and investment banks have been separate ever since. This separation and other tight government regulations characterized banking for the next fifty years.

In 1933 Congress passed the Glass–Steagall Act, one of the most significant laws governing banking. That and other legislation placed severe restrictions on what banks could and could not do. For instance, banks could offer only certain products and types of loans. Legislation also governed how much interest a bank could pay on deposits or charge on loans. What one bank offered was pretty much the same as what every other bank offered. There was little competition, and each bank did business pretty much the same as all other banks.

Deregulation

All this meant that until a few years ago careers in banking were fairly straightforward. You worked in bank operations or in lending and that was it.

Then in the early 1980s banks were deregulated. Banks and banking careers will never be the same again.

Until very recently commercial banks made money on the "spread"—the difference between the interest a bank paid to borrow money and what it charged people who borrowed money from it.

For instance, a bank might pay 4 percent to borrow the money it lent to a homebuyer at 8 percent. The 4 percent spread, or difference between what the bank paid for the money and charged the customer to borrow it, was the bank's profit.

During the days of heavy government regulation, banks made good profits on the spread.

In the early 1980s, however, the interest banks paid to borrow money rose much higher than what they were earning on old mortgages and loans. Profits tumbled. Other kinds of financial service businesses that were not regulated, such as money market mutual funds, began paying investors 14 percent or more on their money. By law, banks could pay only $5^1/_2$ to $5^3/_4$ percent.

What would you do if you were a bank customer and you could get 10 percent more on your money someplace else? That's right: Take your money out of the bank and move it elsewhere. And that is exactly what many depositors did. Money poured out of banks and into other investments.

Consumers put their money in money market mutual funds or interest-bearing checking accounts. Corporate money managers found new ways of financing loans for their companies that were most cost-effective. Suddenly banks began losing deposits, and some banks once again began to fail. This time, deposits were insured by the federal government, so that depositors did not lose their money. Congress again had to act.

Banks needed a way of competing with industries that were not subject to the same regulations they were. But changing the regulations would take time. Meanwhile, banks had to conserve profits or minimize the effects of the losses they were suffering. They started closing branches and cutting staff.

Eventually Congress phased out many of the old regulations so that banks could better compete with nonbank competitors. In 1982, with the passage of the Garn–St. Germain Depository Institutions Act, banks could begin offering services similar to those of their nonbank competitors.

Today banks offer so many services that it would take an entire book to describe them. Computers and advances in electronics have revolutionized banking and led to the creation of new, innovative products and services.

New Products and Services

Banks grow by becoming more profitable. They do that by marketing their products and services and by expanding in certain areas of the marketplace that they have chosen as their own.

Banks began to better define their markets and to market to specific audiences; that is, they identified the products they wanted to sell and the people and organizations that might want to buy those products.

For example, if you decide to start a dog-walking business, you have to market your service. You do that by identifying whom you want for customers. Do you want to walk large dogs or small dogs? Then you have to identify how you can reach people who own the kinds of dogs you want to walk. And you have to convince them you are the best dog walker they can find.

The process is much more complicated for large businesses that have competitors on every corner.

Banks began to search for new products to offer customers, such as foreign exchange trading and home banking. Many banks began to offer discount brokerage services, which enable customers to buy and sell securities without using a broker.

Some banks offer so many products that employees must specialize in specific areas. A customer can open a checking account, make a deposit in a savings account, buy and sell stocks, and invest in an individual retirement account, all under one roof.

The Future of Banking

Over the last few years, banks have begun to invest in new technologies with names like super-ATMs, smart cards, and electronic banking. In fact, American banks spent roughly $20 billion on technology alone in 1996. The technology they are developing is designed to make banking easier and faster for everyone involved.

For instance, banks around the world are testing out a new generation of automated teller machines. The new, super-ATMs can print out instant bank statements, make change, and dispense a wide variety of items, ranging from movie tickets to traveler's checks to stamps. One bank is testing a machine that can print out a customized checkbook on the spot.

The most high-tech ATMs even have two-way videophones that let customers talk to bank officers in a remote, centralized location. Customers at the ATM can fill out a loan or credit-card application on the ATM's touch-sensitive keyboard. If they have any questions, help is just a videophone call away.

Smart cards—also known as digicash or electronic cash cards—are another new invention that banks are testing. A smart card is a small plastic card with a microprocessor computer chip embedded inside it. The cards store the electronic equivalent of cash. For instance, say that you want to buy a candy bar. Instead of paying with cash, you swipe your card over a special terminal at the store counter. The money is automatically deducted from your card. Running out of money on your card? Just take it to the nearest ATM and transfer cash from your checking or savings account to your smart card. No money in your account? Borrow some cash from a friend by transferring it from his or her card to yours. Transfers can also be done by phone or over the Internet.

Smart cards work somewhat like credit cards, but without the costly online verification process that credit cards require. This makes smart cards much cheaper to use. Wells Fargo Bank is trying out a pilot plan by offering smart cards to their employees in San Francisco. The cards can be used at more than twenty different stores. If the plan is successful, smart cards could be available to everyone else in the near future.

One of the most exciting areas in banking right now is electronic banking. Electronic banking allows customers to take care of many of their banking needs by computer. Customers who own a money-management software program and a computer with a modem can dial into the bank's mainframe. There they can check account balances, pay bills, invest in various savings plans, transfer money between accounts, or download bank and credit-card statements.

Some banks are encouraging more people to bank online by offering electronic banking for free while increasing fees for using a teller or ATM. Like ATMs when they were first introduced, electronic banking might take a while for customers to get used to. But banks are counting on the fact that once people see how easy it is to bank with a computer, the technology will take off.

Another recent trend in banking is the use of debit cards. According to *The New York Times* on April 2, 1997, there are more than 60 million debit cards in use. Like a check, a debit card draws money directly from your checking account. For banks, debit cards mean less paperwork and fewer bounced checks. They speed up processing time, because the money is deducted immediately from your checking account. For banks, debit cards are a major step toward paperless banking. A debit card also has advantages for consumers. You don't acquire debt as with a credit card. Many people find debit cards to be convenient, and they like the way that the cards don't cause them to go into debt. There are also no interest charges. Debit cards can make it easier to manage your money.

What advantages do these new technologies offer? Most importantly, speed and convenience. Moving money electronically is much cheaper and faster than moving money by hand. Every ATM transaction costs the average bank roughly twenty-eight cents. Transactions involving a teller cost $1.15 each. The convenience is not only on the bank's side, however. Electronic banking is efficient for customers, too. Instead of standing in line at their local branches, customers will be able to access their accounts whenever they want without leaving home. The end result will be almost like the bank had opened up a personal branch right inside the customer's computer.

Another advantage comes from helping customers feel more in control of their money. By allowing them to take a more hands-on role in their banking, banks will be keeping customers happy. And keeping customers happy, in these competitive times, is necessary for every bank's survival.

The downside to this bright future is the probable decrease in lower-level banking jobs. As more transactions are taken over by computers, fewer clerks and tellers are needed. The arrival of ATMs in the 1980s signalled the first sharp drop in the number of lower-level banking jobs. Over the past decade, while ATM transactions increased by 400 percent, the number of tellers dropped 20 percent. Experts predict that electronic banking, smart cards, and other technologies yet to be developed will reduce the number of tellers even more sharply in the years to come. ATMs have also affected the working hours of bank employees. Banks are open for fewer hours a day than they were in the past, because so many transactions can be handled by ATM.

Bigger and Bigger Banks

Over the last fifteen years, banks began to merge with other banks on an unprecedented scale. This merger mania has resulted in bigger banks, a trend that shows no signs of stopping. Analysts predict that by the end of the decade, the number of commercial banks in the United States will shrink from the current 12,000 to 8,000. As banks are growing larger, banking is rapidly becoming both national and international.

In the past, the McFadden Act of 1927 restricted banks to having branches in their home state. Strictly interpreted, it barred banks from offering interstate banking services, but they got around this restriction by opening loan-processing offices around the country. They also set up subsidiary companies out of state and offered bank card services to out-of-state customers.

Banks often acquire out-of-state branches when a troubled bank is "married" to an out-of-state bank capable of handling a merger. This means that the government requires the troubled bank to merge with another, more solvent bank. So banks have begun to cross state lines.

As the regulations prohibiting interstate banking have been repealed, competition between banks has heated up as they try to lure customers away from each other. This opens up even more career opportunities for employees who want to work in other areas of the country.

Banks are also international businesses. The world has been called a global village. Corporations with international offices must be able to move money and investments from country to country, twenty-four hours a day. International banking helps them do that.

International banking is possible largely because technology has shrunk the world and its time zones into manageable sizes. A Japanese businessman can purchase a California company without leaving his Tokyo office. The entire transaction can be done by phone and computer.

A major function of international banking is making loans to other governments and foreign companies. Starting in the 1970s, commercial banks opened branches overseas to make loans to foreign borrowers. Many of the big players in international banking, such as Citibank, create international syndicates of banks to handle huge transactions for clients. Nowadays, when a company needs financing, an international bank can put together a global package.

Although many U.S. banks have retail banking offices overseas, citizens of the country where the branch is located usually staff the offices. The place for Americans in international banking belongs in the high-finance jobs, and an MBA degree is the key to getting into one of these overseas positions. Some banks also want employees with expertise in foreign languages, especially Japanese.

Career Pathways

Career opportunities in banking have never been more diverse. Bank employees no longer work in just operations or lending. Bank employees are attorneys, computer programmers, marketers, salespeople, economists, research analysts, and fund managers, among dozens of other jobs.

The official workweek ranges from 35 to 40 hours, but most officers work many more hours than that.

Here are some broad areas of banking you can think about:

- *Consumer banking.* This is also called retail banking. You are probably most familiar with the retail bankers. When you go to your local branch,

15

you are dealing with this area of the bank—bankers who serve individuals and small businesses.

- *Commercial banking.* Commercial bankers serve larger businesses and institutions such as schools, governments, unions, and even other banks. They make loans, process employee payrolls, and provide billing services, foreign currency exchange, and funds transfers.
- *Trust banking.* The trust department holds and manages the assets owned by individuals or institutions and manages the money or other assets for the benefit of the customer. For instance, a person can write a will leaving all of his or her assets in trust for heirs. A corporation can set up a trust account for the investment of its employees' pension funds.
- *Operations* and *data processing.* These departments support all the others. They provide record-keeping, bookkeeping, and data processing services for the entire organization. Often, employees work with computers and other equipment.
- *Bank administration* and *accounting.* The administrative employees provide supplies, equipment, personnel, and other support functions for all other units. The accounting department creates and maintains financial records and analyzes the financial health of the company.
- *Public relations* and *marketing.* These employees match customers and their needs with the company's products and services so that the company can make a profit. They research, plan, and implement new products and services and ensure proper delivery to customers. Advertising

and community relations usually fall under these areas.

- *Community banking.* Community banks are the small local banks you find throughout the country. Thirty-five percent of all banking employees nationwide work in community banks. Every employee in a community bank is a generalist and knows many different functions. If you dislike the competitive environment and bustle of a big-city bank, a community bank may be the perfect place for your banking career.

Below, banker Donald Summers provides some helpful advice on careers in the banking field.

Interview: Donald Summers
Chairman, Human Resources Division
American Bankers Association
and Senior Vice President, Security Pacific Bank,
Washington

Q. What is the future for careers in banking?
A. I'm excited by the future of banking, the direction it is taking.

Banking is changing in many ways. It is more sales-oriented than before. Markets are more competitive, and that means that banks have to find ways to sell their services and distinguish themselves from their competitors.

The kinds of jobs that are being created now and that will continue to be created are the more technical sales jobs. In fact, fewer lower-level jobs will be created in the future.

Q. What kind of employees will be needed?
A. It is a time for creativity and creative people. The

most successful person is a broad-based generalist who is flexible and interested in a varied career path.

The most valued positions are going to be sales-oriented jobs. We need people who can put themselves in the shoes of the customer, who can find out what the customer needs and match those needs to a wide array of services and products.

We also need people who can withstand change because change is going to be the norm for a long time to come.

People skills are also very important.

Q. What kind of education will employees need?

A. College is very important. Employees have to be able to absorb a lot of information and present themselves well.

I think a young person who is considering a career in banking should consider a liberal arts degree. We need people with good conceptual skills who can analyze complex information and put it into a format people can understand. As people move up in the organization, they must be able to conceptualize.

We're seeing less emphasis on MBAs. In some cases, the MBA is overeducated for the job, and a graduate degree in business may not serve a person's chosen career. For instance, I obtained my graduate degree in organizational psychology. That was better for me because I had chosen a career in human resources.

It is important get some practical experience in banking before entering a graduate program. Attending graduate school at night is often the best solution.

2

Finance: The World of Wall Street

"Our whole industry has gone through a dramatic change. Originally we were simply stockbrokers; occasionally we did a government or municipal bond. But over the years we have changed our approach. We are no longer called stockbrokers; we are now financial consultants. We tailor the investment vehicle to the needs of the particular client. Our industry is in a far better position now to give the kind of service that the individual investor needs."

William A. Schreyer
Chairman and CEO
Merrill Lynch & Co., Inc.

Wall Street jobs involve buying and selling all kinds of things such as stocks, bonds, commodities, options, and even entire companies. The object of the buying and selling is to make money.

Wall Street.

The words alone bring to mind images of money.

Lots of money.

And power.

The kind of power that goes with lots of money.

And glamour.

The kind of glamour that goes with power and lots of money.

For some people, Wall Street is the American dream.

Wall Street has, in fact, been called the Street of Dreams.

But as sometimes happens, the dream can become a nightmare.

If you saw the movie *Wall Street* or read the newspapers about the many insider trading scandals, you have seen the nightmare side of Wall Street.

It is called greed. It happens when money and power become more important than principles such as honesty, truth, and fair play. People betray the ethics of the business by using privileged information for personal gain.

By far the majority of people working on Wall Street, or in the financial services industry across the nation, are honest, extremely hard-working people. Jobs in finance and investments are some of the most difficult jobs to get and keep. Only the best and the brightest have a shot at the top.

Many people in this business say that they have been interested in investments all their lives. That kind of interest is essential. Many Wall Street jobs place tremendous stress on the people doing them. They are fast-paced, exhilarating, and, sometimes, exhausting.

Some jobs, especially the prestigious jobs in investment banking, require people to work 100 hours a week—more than most other jobs in any other industry.

People burn out young in some of these jobs, but the rewards are as great as the jobs are difficult. Annual salaries for some jobs easily reach six figures. Other jobs bring much lower, five-figure salaries, whereas some give people the opportunity to earn a million dollars a year or more.

But money isn't everything to everyone. There are also the prestige and professional reputation that can be gained by putting together billion-dollar deals.

Wall Street is, literally, a narrow street in lower Manhattan, New York City. It was originally a dirt path with a wall of brush and mud in the Dutch trading post called New Amsterdam. The wall soon became a wooden fence to keep cows from wandering off, but the cows soon gave way to investors.

Wall Street connected the docks on the Hudson River with the docks on the East River. Trade and commerce traveled along Wall Street, as did early merchants who bought and sold furs, money, and tobacco, among other things. Wall Street became a center for much of that trading.

Wall Street coffeehouses and newspapers became the avenues through which investors could buy securities. The first Congress of the United States met in Federal Hall on Wall Street and authorized the issue of $80 million in government bonds.

By 1792 merchants were keeping small inventories of securities to sell over their counters. In that same year twenty-four businessmen signed an agreement to trade securities only among themselves. These men are considered the original members of the New York Stock Exchange (NYSE).

At one time only men worked in Wall Street jobs. The brokerage houses and banks were created by powerful men who gave their business to other powerful men. Many firms were family-owned and passed on from generation to generation. Each firm had its own clientele and territory.

All that has changed. Now most of the old houses and banks are parts of huge conglomerates, such as Prudential Securities.

Deregulation of banking and fixed commissions have blurred the lines and responsibilities between banks and other financial institutions. Competition for customers is keen. New financial products are created—sometimes daily—to lure customers from one company to another.

Many positions cross the boundaries between banking and brokerage. For instance, an analyst covering health care could work for an investment bank, a commercial bank, a brokerage, or an insurance company.

Do you have to go to New York for a "Wall Street" job?

Not necessarily.

Wall Street, USA

Wall Street also symbolizes the financial world of the United States. While the heart of that world *is* the street called Wall in Manhattan, every major city in the country has its "Wall Street," which provides opportunities for sharp, hard-working young people to succeed.

Wall Street, New York, is the capital of the financial services industry and the biggest, most prestigious jobs are there. You can work and live anywhere and be a Wall Street player, but New York is still the financial capital of the world. Most firms require employees to spend at least a few years in New York.

But all the major firms such as Merrill Lynch, Smith Barney, and Dean Witter, major banks such as Citibank and Chase, and many smaller banks and firms have offices in other cities.

Chicago is the center for commodities, and Boston is the home of many mutual funds.

Technology and Wall Street

The explosion of technology has allowed Wall Street to do business in every corner of the world. Face-to-face international conferences are held over phone lines and via satellites. Multimillion-dollar deals are handled by phone, fax, and modem. Computers have shrunk the country and the world to a manageable size. But one unforeseen result of the information surge has been increased competition from an unexpected segment of the population: Wall Street's own clients.

Clients are able to conduct their own research quickly and efficiently on the Internet. Customers of America Online, for instance, can get daily stock quotes. They can also request company profiles, stock reports, financial statements, earnings performance, future earning estimates, and quotes and charts on historical stock performance for thousands of companies. Independent online forums aimed specifically at small investors are filled with stock tips and information about companies and their business prospects.

With all of this information easily available, why would anybody pay hefty charges for a full-service financial adviser? Customers aren't the only ones who are beginning to ponder the answer to that question. Discount online brokerages have recently begun to surface. They charge a minimal fee to buy and sell stocks over the Internet, allowing customers to bypass traditional full-service brokers and their larger fees. By concentrating on making trades instead of gathering advice, the companies keep their costs low. The number of electronic brokerages is expected to multiply rapidly in the next few years. Meanwhile, the big Wall Street firms are beginning to feel the squeeze of competition.

Women and Wall Street
What about women? Do they have a part in today's Wall Street?

Yes.

And no.

One third of all Wall Street pros are women, but few of them hold the big jobs thus far.

That is partly because significant numbers of women began attending graduate schools only fairly recently. In 1974, 7 percent of all MBA graduates nationwide were women. In 1994 women made up 36 percent of the ranks of graduating MBAS.

Proportionately, the number of women on Wall Street is less than men. After the market crash in 1987, 30 percent of the women holding Wall Street jobs were laid off. Most of the women affected had risen to middle-management ranks. Their absence means fewer women mentors for young women just arriving in the profession.

Fewer women than men also seem willing to make the sacrifices many of these jobs entail. Women with families typically have a harder time relocating or spending the 100 hours a week some jobs require.

And prejudice is not uncommon. Despite advances made by the feminist movement, stereotypes die hard, especially in "boy's club" businesses like finance. Many experts believe that there is more sexism on Wall Street than anywhere else. Fortunately, laws exist to protect employees (both male and female) from sexual harassment and discrimination based on sex.

One major Wall Street firm asked female Stanford graduates if they would be willing to have an abortion rather than ruin their career with a pregnancy. An executive of that same firm announced the arrival of new women analysts and associates with a memo adorned by a photo of a seminude woman. Not surprisingly, the firm has been sued for sex discrimination.

A salary survey conducted by Columbia University School of Business also showed that even if male and female MBAS start out with the same qualifications and salaries, at the end of ten years the women are earning

20 percent less than the men. The role of women on Wall Street can be bleak.

But the picture is getting brighter. Today's financial and banking professionals are men and women of all ethnic and cultural backgrounds. As more and more firms look for profits, gender carries less and less weight and talent more and more.

3

Choosing the Right Job in Banking and Finance

This chapter will describe the various job opportunities in the fields of banking and finance. Compare your skills and qualifications to those required for the job. When you find a job that interests you, consider what education and training you will need to obtain to follow that career path.

ACCOUNTANT AND AUDITOR

Accountants analyze, research, prepare, write, and verify the accuracy of financial statements and reports. They may specialize in certain areas such as taxes, accounting systems, and cash flow management.

Management accountants handle the financial records of the companies they work for, such as banks and brokerages. They provide and analyze the financial information their executives need to make sound decisions. They also prepare the financial reports required by the government, stock exchanges, and the Securities and Exchange Commission (SEC). They work in areas such as taxation, budgeting, cash management, treasury, and investments.

Auditors maintain and examine the financial records of a business to verify their accuracy. Internal auditors work for a company and ensure that its financial records are accurate. They also look for areas of waste or where fraud may exist.

Internal auditors objectively weigh a company's internal accounting and compliance procedures to ensure that financial and information systems are accurate and capable of protecting the company from fraud and waste. They review the company's policies and practices to ensure that they meet current laws and government regulations.

Computer software makes these jobs much easier than they previously were. Numbers can be analyzed and printed out in standard formats for reports or rearranged to provide new information. Software reduces the once-tedious work that accountants and auditors had to perform to get the job done.

These jobs require at least a bachelor's degree in accounting or a similar field, and many employers want people with MBAS or CPAS. Familiarity with computers and accounting software is important.

Beginners often start as assistants, ledger accountants, and junior auditors. But even though they are classified as beginners, these employees need practical experience in the area before being hired.

According to the U.S. Department of Labor, employment of auditors and accountants is expected to grow through the end of the century. The complexity of doing business will increase the demand for people who can develop information on costs, expenditures, taxes, and many other types of financial information. This information is especially critical in the areas of business expansion or foreign investments.

CPAS have more opportunities than accountants and auditors without this prestigious designation. In most states, Certified Public Accountants are the only accountants licensed and regulated. The designation is granted when the candidate passes a difficult four-part examination. Most applicants must also have some work experience in the field.

Various professional associations of accountants and auditors grant certifications for members who voluntarily meet each association's requirements.

The Institute of Internal Auditors, Inc. confers the designation Certified Internal Auditor (CIA) on graduates of colleges and universities who have two years of experience in the area and pass a four-part exam.

The EDP Auditors Association confers the designation Certified Information Systems Auditor (CISA) on candidates who complete five years of experience in the field.

The National Association of Accountants (NAA) confers a Certificate in Management Accounting (CMA) on those who pass a series of exams and meet certain standards. The Accreditation Council for Accountancy of the National Society of Public Accountants awards a Certificate of Accreditation in Taxation.

Accountants and auditors need a good aptitude for math and the ability to analyze and interpret facts and figures. They also need clear communication skills in both speaking and writing. Accountants and auditors must work with numbers, reports, and financial statements for long periods of time, so concentration abilities are crucial. Employees also need a high degree of integrity, since important decisions are made based on the accuracy of the reports they complete.

According to a recent salary survey taken by the National Association of Colleges and Employers, beginning accountants and auditors with bachelor's degrees average $27,900 a year; people with master's degrees earn an average of $31,500 a year. Experienced people can earn more than $85,000 a year. CPAS earn even more.

Young people interested in accounting can talk to their college's placement centers about the availability of internships and summer jobs in the field.

BANK TELLER

The teller is the bank employee with whom most customers regularly come into contact. The teller cashes checks; takes deposits; processes withdrawals; sells savings bonds; accepts payments on utility bills, bank charge cards, and loans; processes the paperwork for certificates of deposit; buys and sells foreign currency; and sells traveler's checks.

But that's not all.

Tellers also take deposits from businesses and balance the money deposited against the amount shown on deposit slips. They make up the bags of money that businesses buy to make change for their customers.

As you might guess, a bank teller must be good with numbers. He or she has to count large amounts of cash accurately. A teller must also be able to use computers and other kinds of office equipment such as adding machines.

Bank tellers must also "keep their cool." If the customer also wants to make a deposit, pay a bill, and buy traveler's checks, the teller must apply the same level of accuracy to each transaction. If the customer is in a bad mood, irritated at having to wait in line, or angry over something that has nothing to do with the bank, the teller must also become a master of customer service.

When a customer has multiple transactions, the teller must maintain his or her accuracy while handling a variety of tasks, each requiring a separate set of verifications. For instance, if a customer wants to cash a check, the teller must make sure the written and numerical amounts on the check agree, verify that the person cashing the check is the person to whom it is written,

Bags of coins cover the floor of a bank. An employee uses a forklift to move them to the next stop: machines that will pack them into compact rolls for tellers and merchants (courtesy H. Garfield).

A teller counts out cash to a customer (courtesy American Bankers Association).

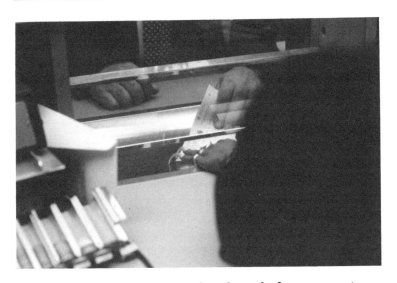

A teller accepts a check for deposit from a customer (courtesy J. Tkatch).

Overhead view of tellers serving customers (courtesy American Bankers Association).

A businesswoman uses an electronic teller machine at San Francisco International Airport (courtesy Matrix).

be certain the account on which the check is drawn has funds to cover the check, and count out the money to the customer.

The teller's day starts before the doors of the bank open, and it ends long after the last customer is helped. Tellers begin the workday by receiving and counting the cash they will work with that day. They are responsible for making sure the cash balances against all the transactions they handle during the day, and balancing their cash is the last thing they do at the end of their shifts.

Some tellers service the automatic teller machines that receive deposits, issue withdrawals, and take payments by computer.

In addition to all this, tellers are expected to sell new services to their customers, so they must be aware of new products and how customers can use them.

The job lends itself to part-time hours, and college students often work as tellers in local banks because of that flexibility. Many bank officers started their career as a part-time teller while in school.

To become a teller, you need good numerical and clerical skills. You must feel comfortable handling large amounts of money and dealing directly with the public. Most tellers have a high school diploma, and many are college students.

Tellers are trained both formally in classes and on the job. They are often paired with experienced tellers, who show them the duties of the job.

Tellers can move on to senior teller positions, and many become customer service representatives. Tellers with some college credits can become managers and supervisors.

Teller jobs are among the lower-paying jobs in banking. According to the U.S. Department of Labor, annual earnings for a full-time teller range from $9,900 to $24,200.

BOOKKEEPER AND ACCOUNTING CLERK

Bookkeepers and accounting clerks keep financial records, either in ledgers or by computer. They also put together financial statements showing the money that a business receives and pays out, including such items as employee salaries, office expenses, and premiums paid to insurance companies. They may also prepare and mail customers' bills and handle inquiries from suppliers.

In large companies several bookkeepers and clerks usually work for more senior staff members. Each clerk may specialize in a certain area such as preparing statements of income from sales, daily operating expenses, or bills paid and due. In a computerized office the clerk or bookkeeper enters the financial information into a computer and reviews and balances printouts based on the information.

Working hours are standard office hours, and these jobs lend themselves to part-time work, so they are good for college students.

Employees usually have at least a high school diploma and must have studied principles of accounting and basic business bookkeeping. Many employers are beginning to require that bookkeepers and accounting clerks also complete an accounting program at a junior college. A knowledge of computers and typing is valuable.

Bookkeepers and accounting clerks must be good with numbers and able to concentrate on detailed work. Even small mistakes can be serious.

Bookkeeping and accounting skills are transferable to most other industries, since just about every business needs bookkeepers and accounting clerks.

The salary for full-time bookkeepers and accounting clerks is $12,600 to $22,400.

BROKER

Brokers are called different things by different companies. Institutional brokers help organizations such as insurance companies, retirement funds, and nonprofit organizations to invest their money.

Brokers who serve individuals are called financial consultants, retail brokers, stockbrokers, or account executives. But no matter what a specific company may call them, they are all registered representatives. That means they have passed the New York Stock Exchange securities examination and are licensed to sell securities. In this section we are talking about brokers who serve individuals.

Fifteen years ago brokers sold stocks and not much else. Today brokers help people buy and sell a wide variety of securities, such as stocks, bonds, shares of mutual funds, gold, silver, tax shelters, money market accounts, mortgage financing, and even insurance.

Brokers advise their clients on how to invest their money to meet their financial goals. They also execute buys and sells for their clients' portfolios.

Most brokers want clients who have at least $50,000 to invest. Some won't represent a client who has less than $100,000 to invest.

Brokers must be certified by several agencies. They must pass an examination that qualifies them to work as a registered representative at the New York Stock Exchange. This is a grueling, six-hour test that can take up to four months to study for.

They also must pass the National Association of Securities Dealers (NASD) test. Many also want commodities and insurance licenses. That means more tests, lots of studying, and, maybe, classes. A broker's firm often helps by supplying study materials and giving or paying for courses.

A bank vault employee inspects an old bond. Older bonds bear coupons that must be clipped and mailed to the paying agent on behalf of the owners of the bonds (courtesy H. Garfield).

Once a broker is registered, the employer sends him or her through an internal training program to learn how the company works. The best training is given in the large supermarket firms such as Merrill Lynch. Typically, newcomers may put in 65 to 70 hours a week just studying and reading about the business and the products and services offered by their company.

After that, brokers are on their own. They are given office space, a desk, a phone, and not much else. Even though brokers work for employers, they can set up their own business and hours. Their goal is to build up a client list and generate income for the company and themselves.

Brokers start out with a salary that gets smaller and smaller and eventually vanishes as their time with the company increases. Eventually, brokers live on commissions only, so if they don't sell they don't get paid.

Every time a client uses a broker, the client is charged a commission. Brokers receive between 30 and 50 percent of the commissions their customers bring into the company. For instance, most brokers are expected to gross at least $200,000 in commissions a year. If the broker earns a 30 percent commission, the annual salary is $60,000 ($200,000 × 30%).

Brokers who bring in the largest gross commissions receive the largest percentages. There is no ceiling on how much a broker can earn. Million-dollar incomes are not uncommon. On the other hand, brokers who consistently bring in below-average gross commissions may find their percentages decreased.

Brokers spend a lot of time looking for leads—people who might be interested in using their services. In the beginning they make lots of "cold calls"—calling total strangers and trying to persuade them to invest. Leads come from lists of high-income people who buy products such as Mercedes Benz or BMW cars or who buy homes in high-income or upscale areas.

Rejection is all too common in this business. Brokers hear a lot of "No's" before someone says "Yes."

Brokers estimate that it takes about three months of customer contact to land a new client. If the broker does a good job, one client will refer the broker to someone else and the broker's book of business will grow. On the average, it takes about two years to build a book of business.

Brokers spend their days on the phone calling leads and their evenings visiting clients at home. Each broker must keep up with what his or her clients need and with new investment products that might meet those needs. Since each broker competes with every other broker on the Street, personal service gives a broker an edge over the competition.

Competition from discount brokerage firms has cut into full-service brokerages. Many investors are also buying and selling securities directly, using their personal computers. This means that brokerages are losing business, and in response some firms are considering paying brokers flat salaries rather than commissions. That could diminish the earnings potential for the job.

Basically, a broker is a salesperson. One of the best qualifications for the job is sales experience, regardless of what was sold. In fact, if a would-be broker has spent several years working as a salesperson and has a good sales record, but doesn't have a college diploma, he or she still has a good chance of getting a broker's job.

Some firms routinely reject all applicants the first time they apply. The firm wants to see persistence on the part of people who really want the job. Applicants are expected to reapply, more than once if necessary, to prove that rejection doesn't stop them.

Interview: George Frankenstein, Vice President
Investment Services Group
Donaldson, Lufkin & Jenrette

Q. How did you become a broker?

A. My dad loved the market, and he always talked to me about it. Even when I was a kid and didn't know what I was talking about, I used to ask him how the market was going. It has always been a part of my life.

When I was in college, I realized I want to be an entrepreneur, to own my own business. My dad suggested that I visit a brokerage firm about a job. I did, and they hired me.

I spent three years working in the back room doing just about everything. I learned it all. Then when I was about twenty-six I finally started selling. I was the kid on the block—the youngest broker in the firm.

I'm also the exception to the rule: I worked my way into the job from the back room. Most of the brokers in this business come from other kinds of jobs, usually sales.

Over the twenty-plus years I've been in this business, I've worked at four different firms and built up a steady, regular list of clients, which I have taken with me. That's the good thing about what I do: You're really self-employed.

Q. Can you give a little more detail on that?

A. The brokerage gives you what you need to set up an office—a space, a desk, a phone; then you're on your own. I even brought my secretary with me from the last move, and I pay her myself.

My clients are mine to take with me if I leave. That's different from being an institutional broker. Accounts are assigned to institutional brokers, but the accounts are clients of the firm, not the broker. If the broker leaves, the clients stay and are assigned to a new broker.

39

This can be a fickle business, and a management change can leave a lot of institutional brokers without a job and clients.

On the other hand, if you are a hot retail broker every brokerage wants you, because you bring your clients with you and can produce commissions immediately.

Q. What do you dislike about the job?

A. This is an information business, and some of that information isn't correct. Sometimes things go sour despite your best intentions. It is very humiliating to tell someone a stock is great based on information you have received, only to have the price drop.

Q. How do you handle the situation when a client loses money?

A. Everybody realizes that there are risks in this business. Sometimes the information you use is bad, or you use bad judgment, or the market in general just drops.

Sometimes you hit it right, and that's the goal: to be right more often than wrong. When you are right, there is no better feeling. I believe that if you are prudent and buy good stocks over a period of time, you will do well.

Q. Do you put together different investments for each client?

A. Yes. The clients' goals are critical. You have to know what they want and what kind of risks they can take.

You also want to be sure you and the client match. You can't be all things to all people.

I'm not a big trader. I try to manage people's money for quality growth and income. For instance, I have a client who is a widow. When I started working with her, we put together a portfolio of stocks for her. Last year I made only one trade for her account. Another broker might have made a dozen.

Q. How can a young person best prepare for a job as a retail broker?

A. This is one of the few businesses you can get into with no capital and do well by doing a good job. But there is one thing you do need: sales experience. Spend four to six years out in the real world after college and sell something. It doesn't matter what, just build up a good sales record.

It's not critical to get a business education. In my opinion, you need only accounting courses so you can read financial statements. You can pick up what else you need to know by reading.

Pick three or four financial publications and read them consistently to build up a bank of knowledge. Learn to talk intelligently about the industry.

You need to create a context for the information you receive. You need a point of reference for making judgments.

I had recommended that a client buy shares of Bank of America stock when it was around $13 a share. The client was so annoyed with the recommendation that he pulled his account. Bank of America stock went down to $7, then the company turned around and the stock is now above $25. I knew Bank of America was going to succeed.

You pick up that kind of knowledge from learning as much as you can about industries and companies. You learn how to make solid judgments. My clients depend on my judgment, and that's a lot of responsibility. You carry the business with you all the time. I never really get a vacation. I call in every day when I'm not here.

Q. Any last advice?

A. If you want to be a broker, become well informed, provide a prudent service over and above the average broker, and keep your customers' needs in mind.

CLERICAL SUPERVISOR AND MANAGER

Clerical support employees keep their companies running smoothly by keeping the paperwork moving. Clerical supervisors and managers interview potential employees and either recommend who should be hired or actually do the hiring. They welcome new employees and orient them the company, and they may also train employees or oversee their training by another employee.

Supervisors and managers must be familiar with the duties of all the jobs that report to them. They make assignments so that the work gets done every day, and they juggle those assignments among employees when someone is absent. So they must understand the strengths and weaknesses of their employees. They also evaluate employee performance and help poor performers improve. They usually can recommend promotions, awards, salary increases, firings, and transfers.

Supervisors and managers monitor workflow to make sure that deadlines are met and that any problems are identified and resolved right away. Most supervisors and managers hold regular meetings with their employees to make sure everyone works toward the same goals.

When problems come up, supervisors and managers take on the responsibility of solving them. That may mean counseling employees with problem behaviors, retraining employees, or changing procedures.

Clerical supervisors and managers report to their managers about how the work is moving and whether their deadlines are being met. No matter what happens, the work must get done. That's their job.

In addition to personnel and workflow matters, clerical supervisors and managers also decide what office equipment their employees need, such as computer terminals, typewriters, and workstations.

If a company is covered by a union contract, the supervisor and manager must understand what is in the contract and abide by its terms in the running of their departments.

Most clerical supervisors and managers work 40-hour weeks, but many take work home to keep current. Often a business requires round-the-clock operation, so some supervisors and managers work swing or grave-yard shifts and many draw extra pay for night work.

These jobs are not entry-level positions. Most clerical supervisors and managers are promoted from within the company or are recruited from other companies. They must demonstrate a solid knowledge of job duties and the ability to supervise people, follow orders, deal with stress, and balance the needs of their managers and their employees.

Good supervisors and managers are efficient and use time to their advantage. They organize work and set priorities well. Many have bachelor's degrees, and most larger companies either offer in-house developmental classes or reimburse supervisors and managers for the fees they pay for outside classes.

Salaries range from $16,300 to $47,200.

COMMERCIAL BANKER

While commercial banks move into new areas such as discount brokerage, insurance, and investments, most banks still concentrate on lending or wholesale banking.

Government organizations, domestic and foreign countries, and private corporations are typical customers who use a wide variety of banking services, often borrowing money to finance their growth. They need bank accounts that allow them to deposit money and earn interest on it while it is not in use. They also use a bank to process and issue paychecks for their employees.

Commercial bank loan officers are key players in maintaining good customer relationships. They determine a customer's creditworthiness—the customer's ability to pay back borrowed money. They do this by studying a company's financial statements, its position in the industry, and many other factors.

Loan officers work closely with customers to determine their financial needs so they can sell them bank products and services that meet those needs.

Loan officers in most banks specialize in a certain kind of customer, such as small businesses, foreign governments, cities, and domestic corporations. Some bankers specialize in industries, for instance, the auto industry or real estate. Entire groups within the bank may be organized to serve these customers.

In the international area bankers also handle the financial needs of foreign companies and domestic companies that have overseas units. Part of their job is to protect their clients from the adverse effects of foreign currency exchanges.

Many banks have what is called a new business group. The employees in this area actively look for new businesses to which they can sell the bank's products and services. They rely less on cold calls (calling strangers to ask for business) than on obtaining recommendations from existing customers or their current contacts.

Competition is keen among banks, and it is necessary for each bank to set itself apart from the others. That means providing personal service. So commercial bankers may entertain their clients with lunches, dinners, and tickets to events.

Most financial services companies offer training programs for commercial banking. The program may last a few months to a few years, and it may rotate trainees in all positions or put each trainee in a specific area for the entire training period.

Some banks design training programs to eliminate the bottom 10 percent of the class; other banks want to keep all their trainees. It is important to find out the nature of the program and its attrition rate for new trainees.

Salaries start in the low teens for trainees and move up at a steady if not spectacular rate. You will need a bachelor's degree and an MBA if you are interested in foreign banking.

Interview: Wesley Low, Assistant Vice President
Real Estate
Union Bank

Q. What is your background?
A. I have a BS degree in finance and urban land use affairs. Appraising is highly specialized. Most people learn appraising on the job.
Q. What do you do?
A. I am a staff appraiser. I appraise property that is collateral for a loan. Union Bank is a construction lender, so I appraise something that isn't built yet. I look at the plans and try to visualize what it would be worth if it were already built. The bank needs that information to decide whether it will lend money on the project. I'm the loan officer's eyes and ears.
Q. What do you have to know to perform appraisals?
A. You wear a lot of hats. You have to think like a tenant, the developer, an investor, the leasing agent, the architect.

You have to be able to read leases and contracts, survey the market, research the demand for the type of structure being constructed, read plans, determine what the building will rent for. That's just part of what you have to research before you can submit your conclusions to the loan department.

You are an investigator, building a case and supporting what you believe is the value.

The bottom line is that you are expressing an opinion. Sometimes you have to argue it with the loan officer or the leasing agent.

Q. Does the job end after the appraisal is done?

A. No. If the bank makes the loan you monitor the project, and if the building doesn't lease up you have to reappraise it.

And it doesn't end at the end of the day. Because I'm in construction, I tend to evaluate how everything is built or made, from the booths in the restaurant where I eat dinner to the carpeting in a friend's apartment house lobby.

Q. How did you start in the business?

A. I started appraising four-plexes, then moved into commercial and industrial properties.

Q. How far can you go?

A. Some appraisers obtain a professional designation from the American Institute of Real Estate Appraisers or the Society of Real Estate Appraisers. After that, they open their own business or become a chief appraiser and run the department. Some become consultants, performing feasibility studies.

Q. What do you like about the job?

A. Job satisfaction comes from knowing your market and being able to substantiate what you believe. I like analyzing the data and finding hard evidence to support my opinion.

You're constantly in the market, talking to brokers, buyers, and sellers. Every property is different.

The hours are flexible. You spend a lot of time in the field, although residential property appraisers spend more time outside than commercial appraisers do.

COMMODITY TRADER

Commodities are the things that make the world go round. Sugar, salt, wheat, gold, corn, coffee, hogs, cattle, silver, lumber, oil—the list is almost endless. And savvy investors buy and sell each and every one of these items, hoping to make a profit.

Commodities trading began in 1848 when eighty-two businessmen formed the Chicago Board of Trade. The heart of commodities trading is still in Chicago, but anyone, anywhere, can trade in commodities.

Commodities, more than any other investment, depend on circumstances such as weather, natural disasters, and world events. A drought in the Midwest may mean that farmers grow less wheat. The price of wheat soars. A military coup in a coffee-growing country sends coffee prices soaring. An oil spill in Alaskan waters pushes up the prices of oil and gasoline.

Commodities involve futures and options.

When a producer sees a book he thinks will make a good movie, he options it. That means he buys the rights to make a movie from the book by a certain date in the future. While the option is in effect, no one else can make a movie from that book. If the movie isn't made, the option can be renewed or dropped. If it is dropped, another producer can option it.

The commodities market operates similarly. You buy an option to buy a commodity at a certain future date. It is like placing a bet that the price for your commodity will go up or down. If you think it will go up, you buy a *call* option. If you think it will go down, you sell a *put* option.

With a futures contract, you decide to buy or sell a specific amount of a certain commodity by a set date in the future.

This is how commodities investing works:

Let's say you buy wheat from a farmer, then sell it

47

to a baker. Your profit comes from the spread, the difference between what you paid for the wheat and what you sell it for. If you buy the wheat at $2.00 a pound, but the wheat crop that year is very good, you might have to sell it for $1.50 a pound because everyone else is selling wheat too and the price has been driven down. In this case, you lose money—50 cents on the pound. On the other hand, if the wheat crop is thin that year, wheat is at a premium and you might be able to sell it for $3.00 a pound. Now you make a profit.

You can also buy the right to buy wheat the farmer hasn't grown yet. You promise to pay a certain amount of money for the wheat at harvest time, hoping you can sell it for a higher price when the time comes. That is futures trading.

Or you can buy an option. You pay the farmer 25 cents a pound for the right to buy his wheat for a specific amount per pound within a certain amount of time. He keeps your option money whether you buy the wheat or not.

As you can see, commodities are pretty tricky investments. But investors can make a million dollars on one smart move.

Commodity traders have seats on commodities exchanges. The number of seats is limited, and the price of a seat is usually several hundred thousand dollars. Buying a seat gives the trader the right to buy and sell commodities without using a broker and paying commissions.

Traders can lease a seat for $60,000 to $70,000.

The trading floor is called The Pit, and it is a no-holds-barred place. Polite behavior and manners have no place in The Pit. It is a rough-and-tumble environment.

Newcomers start out in The Pit as runners and clerks,

earning between $5,000 and $35,000 a year. After they learn the ropes, they can buy or lease a seat. They also need about $25,000 in cash to trade for their own account.

Traders use a clearing agent, who charges them per contract and who functions as a bank. The agent provides capital, an office, and secretarial support and may even give traders employee benefits.

Traders specialize in certain commodities, often buying and selling contracts within minutes of each other. They can make a fortune one minute and lose it the next.

Traders often make six-figure incomes—not bad for a job that does not require a college degree.

COMPUTER OPERATOR

Years ago a company's computer occupied an entire room. Today entire rooms are still devoted to data processing, but the computers are smaller, lighter, and faster than ever before.

Computers allow financial businesses and banks to store and manipulate millions of pieces of information and documents online. Perhaps more than any other recent innovation, computers have made international banking and finance a reality.

People thousands of miles apart can conduct extremely sophisticated transactions without leaving their offices. Computers can be used to itemize accounts, create research reports, quote the prices of securities worldwide, and project results of investments based on several variables.

On the New York Stock Exchange 100 million shares are traded each day. Computers handle it all.

This means that career opportunities have never been

More and more information is kept on computers. Here, two employees check the accuracy of the information on the computer screen (courtesy H. Garfield).

better for computer operators and operators of peripheral equipment such as printers and disk drives.

In small companies computer operators may be expected to take care of all the peripheral equipment. In larger companies the peripherals are maintained and run by peripheral equipment operators. The tasks of both jobs are similar.

Operators load the tapes, disks, and paper into the equipment and monitor the machines running the data. Some computer runs last twenty-four hours, for instance, when a bank runs the bills for its credit card customers or when a large company's payroll checks are run.

Computer and peripheral equipment operators monitor the equipment, handle any problems that arise, and respond to any error messages that occur. It is the operator's responsibility to locate the problem and either solve it or end the program.

Because some programs run for twenty-four hours, most computer operator jobs involve shift work, and they are often staffed seven days a week. In addition to businesses in banking and finance, most industries that must maintain large amounts of customer or employee data—such as insurance companies, hospitals, and colleges—use computer operators. The job offers the opportunity to change employers and industries.

Many companies train computer operators on the job, and clerical workers from other areas have the opportunity to transfer into this area. Many high schools, vocational schools, business schools, and community colleges offer courses in computer operations.

Most employers want people with at least a high school diploma. Some prefer employees with data processing experience.

Salaries range from $12,800 to $39,500 a year.

DATA ENTRY KEYER

Data on computers must be updated daily and sometimes hourly. When a bank customer writes a check or makes a deposit, the information must be entered in his or her account with the bank. When someone buys or sells stock, the transaction must be entered in the client's account with the brokerage.

Information on employees, customers, and even the competition is often maintained on a company's computers, and it is the job of data entry keyers to make sure that the information is kept current.

The data entry keyer types information from various documents directly into the computer. Keyers work with video display terminals, which can lead to eyestrain. Equipment is similar to a typewriter.

Some operators enter the information directly online. Other operators use equipment that converts the information into magnetic impulses, which are read into the computer later.

Many businesses offer data entry keyer jobs, and the skills are easily transferred from one employer to another. Most employers require a high school education and the ability to key information at a certain speed.

Data entry keyers earn an average of $17,600 per year.

Economist

Economists study how a society uses resources such as labor, raw materials, and machinery to produce goods and services, and they look at the benefits and costs of distributing and using these goods and services.

Economists use mathematical theories to explain the reasons for business cycles or inflation, to predict the effects of events such as taxation or unemployment, or study and analyze consumer spending trends. They then use their theories to advise businesses in many industries, including banking and finance.

Economists, to a certain extent, try to predict the future based on existing information and trends. Some types of predictions they may be asked to make involve what new products and services should be developed and how they should be priced and marketed; how a company should diversify its operations; whether a new branch should be opened; and the forecast of foreign or domestic economic conditions.

Economists obtain the information they need to make their recommendations and forecasts in several ways. They may conduct surveys; develop models for projections; review and analyze reports, articles, tables, statistics, charts, and any other pertinent documents;

and interview experts in those areas. They then put together reports of their results in clear, readable terms.

Often, economists work under great pressure and tight deadlines, juggling several research reports at one time.

Most economists work for private companies such as banks, investment firms, brokerages, and insurance companies. Most work in large cities, usually in the home offices of their companies, since their work directly affects decisions made at the highest levels of the organization.

Beginning economists need a bachelor's degree in either economics or marketing, with courses in microeconomics, macroeconomics, business cycles, economic and business history, economic development, money and banking, and marketing among others. A strong background in mathematics, statistics, survey design, and computer science is helpful. Advancement to senior economist positions requires a graduate degree in economics. Starting salaries average around $25,400 per year for economists with a bachelor's degree in marketing and around $27,600 per year for those with a bachelor's degree in economics. Economists with a Ph.D. can earn more than $80,000 a year.

The U.S. Department of Labor projects that the need for economists will grow faster than many other occupations through the end of the century. The best opportunities can be found in the financial services industry, which also pays the highest salaries.

FILE CLERK

Despite the wide use of computers, files must still be maintained in all businesses. File clerks are responsible for maintaining and updating accurate records. They classify, store, update, and retrieve material and identify and file new material.

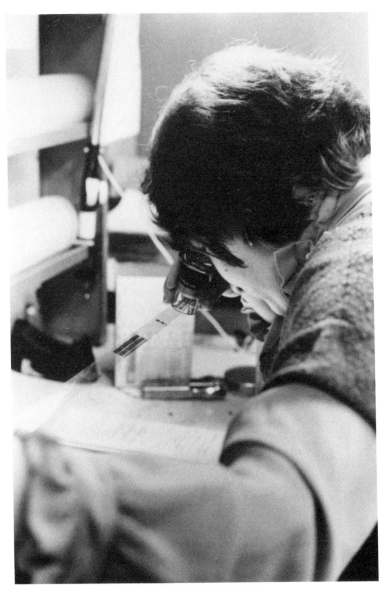

An employee inspects the quality of a microfilmed document (courtesy H. Garfield).

Files can be maintained by subject, by alphabetical order, or by numerical order. Files are usually maintained in either a paper or microfilmed format.

File clerks may also perform miscellaneous clerical duties such as typing, photocopying, or opening, sorting, and posting mail.

File clerks must be able to type and do accurate paperwork. Good spelling is essential, as is neatness.

Employers prefer candidates with high school educations. Training usually occurs on the job, since each company has its own system.

File clerk jobs are entry-level positions, and most employers look for people who demonstrate an ability to learn, assume additional responsibilities, and, eventually, move on to other jobs.

Annual earnings average around $16,200.

FINANCIAL MANAGER

Financial managers are called by a variety of titles such as treasurer, controller, or cash manager according to their primary responsibility.

Because banks and other financial services companies handle so much cash and securities, financial managers are needed in many areas. Managers must be totally familiar with the laws and regulations governing the industry and their particular area. They must also have a working knowledge of other areas, and some need a thorough understanding of the financial systems, laws, and regulations of foreign countries.

Basically, financial managers prepare the financial reports a company issues to comply with laws and government regulations and oversee the flow of cash into and out of a company.

In large firms financial managers may also consult with other managers, lawyers, economists, and other financial professionals to develop, implement, and monitor financial policies and procedures.

The *controller* manages the accounting, audit, and budget departments and directs the research and preparation of financial reports such as income statements and balance sheets.

Cash managers control the flow of money. They monitor and recommend investments of the company's money to ensure that financial goals are met.

Risk and *insurance managers* minimize losses and risks that come from the financial transactions in which the company engages.

Credit managers establish credit criteria and monitor the company's use and extension of credit.

A bachelor's degree in accounting, finance, or business is required, and with many employers an MBA is essential for advancement. A knowledge of computers and a variety of financial services such as banking, insurance, and securities is important.

Most often, financial managers work their way up in the organization, although a company may hire an experienced financial manager from a competitor if no qualified candidate is available internally. Good candidates for financial manager jobs are accountants; budget, credit, or securities analysts; and loan officers.

Experienced financial managers can work in just about any industry, so the opportunity to move around and advance is good. Many financial managers also establish their own consulting firms.

The U.S. Department of Labor estimates that the need for financial managers will grow over the next few years, especially as competition, government reporting regulations, and the complexity of financial services increase. Competition for the best jobs will also be keen.

Annual salaries range from $20,000 or less to more than $77,800. Many financial managers also receive bonuses that can double their income.

Financial Planner

Financial planning is a fairly new career path. It began in the 1960s, but it was not until 1972 that the nation's first financial planning curriculum was established with the College for Financial Planning.

When the banking industry was deregulated, banks introduced a variety of financial products to lure customers away from their competitors. Nonbank industries such as insurance companies, stockbrokers, and even retailers introduced investment products and services.

Today's financial environment is much more complicated than ever before, and investors must understand inflation, changing tax laws, the need for retirement planning, complicated employee benefit plans, and thousands of financial products—or hire professionals who do understand them.

The average person cannot begin to know all the options available. That is where the financial planner comes in. There are too many variables for the average person to take into account.

Financial planners help people invest their money. They analyze a client's financial status and fitness and create an investment plan to help the client reach his or her financial goals. A plan can include ways to lower taxes, increase investment income, provide adequate insurance coverage, and plan for retirement income.

According to Dr. William L. Anthes, president of the College for Financial Planning, in Denver, Colorado, "To accommodate the needs of various clients and understand the sophisticated array of financial products available in the marketplace, a financial planner must have both technical training and professional experience."

In a survey of financial planners conducted by the College, respondents stated that the most important subjects that planners needed to master were listening and speaking skills, knowledge of ethical standards and practices, financial planning and investment planning processes, and tax laws.

The financial planner may be a generalist, trained in many different areas. He or she must understand insurance, taxes, employee benefit plans, investments, individual retirement accounts, and trust funds among other financial programs and products. A financial planner can also coordinate the work of other financial professionals such as accountants, tax attorneys, lawyers, and bankers.

Often a planner has a degree in accounting, economics, business administration, or finance. Planners who deal in securities must have a license or be registered with the Securities and Exchange Commission or the National Association of Securities Dealers (NASD).

Planners who handle insurance products should be licensed by the Division of Insurance or a similar agency for the state in which the planner does business.

According to the College for Financial Planning, career opportunities are "seemingly endless." You can specialize in any number of areas such as accounting, insurance, securities, banking, or law.

You can practice anywhere in the country. The five top states where financial planners practice are California, Texas, Florida, New Jersey, and Pennsylvania. You can work independently or with a company.

No federal standards govern financial planners. Anyone can call himself a planner and advertise for clients. But there are professional organizations that require a level of education and professional expertise before admitting planners to membership.

Just about everyone needs a financial plan of some kind. The simplest plan is a budget. Generally, the more money one earns, the more financial decisions must be made. Most people work for employers that provide employee benefit plans, which require more decisions. Truly wealthy people have fortunes to protect and multiply.

A client consults a financial planner for many reasons:

- to choose investments for a specific goal such as a child's college education, a home down payment, or a retirement nest egg;
- to reduce taxes;
- to obtain the right amount and kind of insurance protection;
- to integrate employee benefit plans with personal investment and insurance plans;
- to maximize investment earnings;
- to organize finances.

Many planners specialize. Some handle only wealthy or upscale clients with a financial worth of several hundred thousand dollars. Others work with people just starting their careers. Many are self-employed; some work for corporations or small businesses that specialize in certain areas of finance.

A planner pulls together all the client's financial information and future goals by working with the client to complete a detailed questionnaire. The planner must know exactly where the client is financially and where the client wants to go.

The planner also must assess each client's "risk quotient"—the ability to handle risk. Some clients want only very safe investments such as government bonds and insured savings vehicles such as time certificates of deposit.

Other clients are willing to take large risks such as providing capital for start-up businesses or investing in the options market.

Most people probably fall in between and are willing to run the risks associated with investing in stocks and bonds, mutual funds, and other uninsured, but relatively safe, investments.

The planner then studies all this information and puts together an investment plan. The plan includes recommendations for financial investments, insurance, and taxes. But that is not the end of it.

The planner must constantly update the financial plan as the economy and the client's personal situation change to make sure that the plan remains true to the client's goals and accurately reflects the client's financial status.

Some planners merely complete the plan; others help the client to implement it by actually making the investments and purchasing the products they have recommended.

The average annual salary for a planner is $37,300, but some planners earn more than $120,000 a year. Financial planners earn their income in several ways. Some charge hourly or flat fees. Some promote certain products and services and are paid a commission when they sell those products to investors. Others combine both commissions and fees.

Flat fees vary according to the complexity of the plan. If you work for a company, the plan usually takes into account investment or insurance products offered by your employer.

The program offered by the College for Financial Planning teaches all areas of personal financial planning. It is a two-year course of study leading to the professional designation. This program was the nation's first formal financial planner program and has earned widespread recognition and respect.

The College for Financial Planning offers several degrees, including a designation of Certified Financial Planner (CFP). After completing the course, graduates receive the CFP designation from the Institute of Certified Financial Planners. After the degree is granted, members must complete at least thirty additional units of study each year.

Most candidates already have college degrees. To qualify for the program, you must have at least three years of professional experience in personal financial planning or a closely related area of the financial services industry such as insurance, banking, accounting, or investment. If you have less than three years of experience, you can enroll with provisional status until you fulfill the three-year requirement.

Many colleges and universities also offer courses, certificates, and undergraduate and graduate programs in financial planning and investments.

A candidate for a financial planning program needs a knack for detail work, a sense of organization, good problem-solving skills, the ability to work well with people, and good listening and communication skills.

Most of the planners enrolled in the College of Financial Planning hold bachelor's degrees, and some have received graduate degrees. Degrees in accounting, finance, business, or a related area provide a good foundation. However, some students enrolled in the CFP program have only a high school diploma, so it is possible to become a planner without a formal college education. The College also offers a paraplanner program for people who provide support services to planners.

Interview: Violaine D'Amour
Master's Degree in Financial Planning

Violaine D'Amour has a master's degree in financial planning and is an enrolled agent. Enrolled agents have passed a difficult test on taxes and can represent their clients in tax courts. She is also an active member of the International Association of Financial Planners, serving as chair of the Scholarship Committee and Vice President of Education.

Q. What was your background before becoming a financial planner?

A. I loved numbers all my life. As a child I used to memorize license plates!

While I was studying for my bachelor's degree, I worked for a bank, analyzing real estate portfolios. I liked the numbers and working one-on-one with people.

One day I went to an orientation for graduate programs at a local university and discovered that there was a program for financial planning. I could work with numbers in a way I loved! I enrolled full time and completed my course of study in 10 months.

Q. Why does a person use the services of a financial planner?

A. Clients often feel lost when it comes to financial planning. They don't know what to do and they don't have the time to do it.

You have to be able to communicate people's financial status and plans to them in a way that is not intimidating, a way that does not put them off.

A good planner is not a broker. We are money doctors. In fact, I think financial planning is a counseling job. I'm almost a money psychologist.

I once had a client with $7,000 in credit card debt. He used his cards to raise his self-esteem. We worked on that issue, and he eventually changed the way he used credit.

Q. How does the planning process work?

A. You have to show people where they are financially.

I ask lots of questions. I have to know their age so we can determine when they will retire. I want to know the life-style they want now and at retirement. Do they work for someone else, or are they self-employed? Things like that.

I have to put together a picture of how the client uses money. I construct a year's budget, showing where the money will come from and where it will go.

If the plan shows that the person is spending more money than he or she is bringing in, the person must either earn more money—which can be very hard—or cut expenses—which can also be very hard!

Q. How did you start your business?

A. I marketed myself by doing financial plans for $1.00. My name got out. Then I put on seminars and taught a class. Clients began recommending me to their friends, and my business grew.

Q. What kinds of fees do planners charge?

A. My clients pay me a yearly retainer that covers all my services. I base it on what my clients need. Some of my colleagues charge $90 an hour, and there are planners charging $165 an hour.

Q. What is the future for financial planners?

A. I think financial planning is a very promising field, especially for people who want to help others with their savings, who want to see the results of their planning come true.

Q. What does it take to be a planner?

A. You have to like people *and* numbers. You should study math, finance, investments, psychology, writing, English, and economics.

You can get a certificate in planning or a bachelor's degree. However, a master's degree sets you apart.

HUMAN RESOURCES

Matching the best employees to available jobs is important to a company's success. Human resources professionals establish policies and procedures for employment, compensation, benefits, and training.

In companies where employees are represented by unions, the human resources professionals may be involved in contract negotiations, and they may represent the company in grievance hearings. In companies without union representation, human resources professionals often act as liaisons between employees and management.

The ability to deal with people at all levels of the company is a critical skill.

Recruiters: Recruiters scout college campuses and other companies for potential employees. They often travel around the country to speak to qualified people to fill vacancies. They must be thoroughly familiar with the company so they can evaluate a prospective employee's skills relative to jobs. They must also be able to discuss all personnel policies, training programs, and promotional opportunities within the company.

Equal Employment Opportunity (EEO) representatives: These employees ensure that plans to hire and promote minority employees are implemented. They resolve EEO grievances, look for violations of anti-discrimination policies, and submit EEO reports.

Job analysts: Analysts compile information on job duties so that detailed job descriptions can be prepared. These descriptions also include information on the training or skills required to do the job.

Compensation managers: Compensation managers develop a company's pay policies and ensure that the company is competitive and can hire the best employees. They conduct salary surveys to see where the company's salaries are relative to other companies.

Benefits managers: Benefits managers design employee benefit programs to attract and retain qualified employees. This can include putting together cost-effective health care, life insurance, disability, and retirement programs for employees at all levels of the company. The benefits area is highly regulated, and benefits managers must understand how various laws and regulations affect their plans and companies.

Training managers: Training managers design programs to train new employees, to retrain employees whose jobs are eliminated, and to develop management potential. Training can be technical, designed to teach skills needed to perform specific jobs, such as lending or analyzing stocks. It can also be general, such as time management or supervision.

In large companies many different employees perform these duties, but in small companies one or two people may be responsible for all of them.

A bachelor's degree is necessary for most jobs. Exposure to liberal arts, psychology, business, and economics is important, but the choice of major is not critical. Many companies maintain personnel records on computers, and human resources employees should be familiar with computers and data processing.

Yearly salaries vary widely by type of job and company, ranging from less than $18,000 to more than $100,000 paid to senior people who direct entire functions within the human resources area.

INSTITUTIONAL BROKER

Institutional account executives are brokers to companies and institutions with large amounts of money to be invested and large portfolios to be managed. They act as middlepersons between customers and the research analysts who work for the investment company. They are assigned to a variety of customers such as mutual funds, retirement funds, and trust funds. Their customers belong to the company they work for; if the broker leaves, the customers are reassigned to another broker.

The account executive recommends which stocks and bonds to buy for the institution's portfolio, based on the research done by the analysts. Part of the account executive's job is to visit clients regularly and encourage them to buy the securities recommended by the research analysts.

The buys and sells are executed by the brokerage, which earns a commission on the transactions. One of the account executive's goals is to earn commissions for his or her brokerage.

If an analyst's opinions on a stock change, the account executive immediately notifies his or her customers with recommendations either to buy or to sell the stock. Unlike retail brokers who specialize in certain stocks or industries or other kinds of investments, institutional brokers must be generalists. They need to be familiar with all the stocks the company's research analysts follow. In some companies that can mean thousands of different stocks. A new account executive can spend months reading research reports.

Electronic technology such as computers, modems, and FAX machines have made it easier for institutional clients to deal directly with a brokerage's research analysts. Some experts think this trend will make the broker's job less important in the future.

An MBA is usually required, and salaries can top $300,000 a year. Top brokers can earn over a million dollars.

Investment Banker

Investment banking is *the* job in banking and finance. It is the most glamorous, the most competitive, the most difficult job to get.

Investment bankers help businesses grow. As a company grows, it usually reaches a time when it needs more money than it can raise on its own. The company may not want to borrow from a bank because it does not want to incur a debt that must be paid back with interest. Instead, the company wants to raise permanent capital by issuing stocks or bonds. (Bonds are debts, but usually the company has many more years to repay the debt than it has with a bank loan.)

Investment bankers help companies raise capital. Traditionally, investment bankers match companies that need money with companies that want to invest money. Their jobs and their clients take them around the world.

The investment banker may decide that a private placement is called for. Capital is raised by making an offer to a private investor or investors.

Investment bankers also help take companies public. They help their client companies raise money by issuing shares of stock or bonds or packages of both. The bankers decide when to go public and what to charge for the securities.

These securities are sold to individuals who buy only a few hundred shares or to institutions that may buy thousands of shares. The result can bring millions of dollars of capital to the client company.

The investment banker decides what is the best solution to the client's problem. Once a decision is made, the investment bank handles the transactions. They prepare the legal documents required, and file them with the government and securities agencies. These documents must be completely accurate. There is no room for error, and an important, time-consuming part of the process involves researching, writing, and managing the printing and filing of these documents.

Investment banking is a team activity. Each team is made up of three to five people, including analysts, associates, and a managing director. Analysts and associates (entry-level employees) may work on more than one team. They gather and compile most of the information needed for the offering, double- and triple-checking the numbers until they are certain they are correct. The team also works closely with the company's legal and accounting staffs.

Usually, larger team is also formed. Called a syndicate, it is made up of other investment banks invited by the original bank to participate in the venture. Each member bank of the syndicate agrees to underwrite a certain amount of the securities being offered. Underwriting banks guarantee payment for the securities.

The originating investment bank may form yet another team called a selling group. The selling group is made up of other investment banks and brokerages that agree to help sell the securities. The selling group does not guarantee that the securities will be sold.

Once all the government and state approvals are granted, the offering is made to the institutional and retail clients of the underwriting investment banks and the banks and brokerages in the selling group.

Part of the selling effort involves going on the road. Investment bankers and institutional brokers tour major cities and give presentations on the offering to institutional investors.

Because the Glass–Steagall Act bars banks from underwriting securities, they engage in investment banking only to underwrite noncorporate securities. For example, a commercial bank may underwrite a bond issue to finance a city library or a new facility on a college campus. They can also give investment advice and arrange for private placements. Banks compete with brokerages and investment banking firms that can, by law, offer a full range of investment banking services.

Investment bankers make money on the spread, the difference between what they pay for the securities and what they sell them for. They make a profit if the price of the security exceeds what they paid for it in the days following the offering. They can also realize a loss if the price falls below the original buying price. Millions of dollars can be gained or lost in a day.

Today investment bankers also offer advice on mergers and acquisitions—takeovers of one company by another. They give financial advice to companies that want to sell a subsidiary or division, and to governments and foreign countries.

No one does everything; there is too much to know for one person to be able to handle it all. Some investment bankers specialize in certain types of business such as mergers and acquisitions, private placements, or real estate. Some bankers are generalists and become experts in certain industries such as health care. Public finance specialists work with governments and municipalities.

The business of investment banking is complicated, the environment in which the bankers work is highly competitive, and their primary business is selling their services.

Today investment bankers are salespeople. They must develop relationships with customers and potential clients, and they must cultivate existing relationships. Millions of dollars are to be made, and each investment bank wants a piece of that wealth.

According to Meryl Gordon, former economics reporter for Gannett News Service, "With potential fees so high, investment bankers aren't content just to sit back and wait for business to come in—they go out and make it happen, searching out undervalued companies and touting them to likely acquirers, setting the wheels of merger in motion. While their gyrations may destroy thousands of jobs and devastate entire communities, these Wall Street dealmakers are totally sheltered from the consequences of their actions. It's an amoral game: Whoever ends up with the most deals and dollars wins." *

Thousands of the best and brightest graduates of the nation's best business schools compete for a handful of jobs each year. The top ten investment banks receive 4,000 résumés a year. They hire only two dozen MBAS and even fewer undergraduates.

What is so wonderful, so attractive about a business that requires people to work eighty to 100 hours a week, week in and week out?

Glamour.

Prestige.

The chance to make a million-dollar income.

Investment bankers earn millions of dollars on billion-dollar deals. For instance, when Philip Morris bought out General Foods for $5.6 billion, the three investment banks that put the package together split $24.3 million in commissions. An investment banker's bonus can *easily double* his or her salary.

That kind of money can be tempting to some, and investment banking has recently reeled under the impact of major insider trading scandals.

The information that financial people obtain about companies or securities cannot be used for personal

---

* Gordon, Meryl. "The Baby Bankers." *Rolling Stone*, 9–25–86.

gain until that information is made public. Nor can the information be given to someone else to use for gain. When this rule is violated, the federal government is swift to prosecute the violators.

Financial companies work hard to make sure that insider information does not pass between their investment banking and trading departments to ensure that insider trading laws are not broken.

You can come to investment banking from three directions: directly from college as an analyst; with an MBA; or transferring in from the legal, management consulting, or accounting fields.

The investment banking entry-level jobs offer one of the steepest learning curves on Wall Street. And while some companies offer formal training, much of the work is learned on the job; you either sink or swim.

Analysts (entry-level positions for recent college graduates) can earn $30,000 a year to start. Bonuses can raise that to a whopping $50,000 by the end of the analyst's second year.

The analyst position was designed by Morgan Stanley less than thirty years ago. Other firms quickly picked up the idea. The job offers recent college graduates with a bachelor's degree the opportunity to spend two years with an investment bank before returning to school for their MBAS. This is one job in which you cannot go to school at night. You will be working most nights.

Almost any undergraduate field of study will do for the analyst program. In fact, many recruiters prefer liberal arts majors. But do not neglect a few computer, accounting, and business courses. They give you the edge in this highly competitive arena.

Research analysts are the gofers of investment banking. Usually, each analyst is part of three- or four-person teams, with each team working on a different project.

The analyst spends lots of time crunching numbers. Part of the job is to analyze a company and its position in its industry. That means studying endless financial reports and accounting records.

Analysts also perform secretarial duties. They proofread documents and spend hours at photocopying machines putting together reports.

Some companies move their analysts around, exposing them to various specialties. In other companies, they stay in the area where they start.

Despite the money and prestige, many analysts drop out of the program. As one dropout says, "I was prepared to work like crazy. What I wasn't prepared for was working around the clock *and* being bored to tears by what I was doing."

To continue in investment banking, most people need an MBA. A few rare superstars are offered associate positions directly out of their analyst training.

Most MBA programs prefer candidates who have had practical business experience, and the analyst programs offered by investment banks fill that requirement nicely.

New MBAS arrive as junior members and join the ranks of the gofers for their first year or two. Then they move up and begin to take on more responsibility.

MBAS start between $60,000 and $80,000 and usually make more than $100,000 by the end of their second year. You can get a vice presidency and make $300,000 (or a million if you are very good) by age thirty.

The grueling, demanding hours and hard work do not lighten up, however, as you move up in the firm. That is one reason investment banking has been called a young person's business. It takes youth to handle the stress and labor involved.

What does it take to be an investment banker?

Grades: You need the best grades in both undergraduate and graduate schools.

Leadership: You must show leadership in sports, campus government, or other college activity.

Balance: You must show strong skills in both analytic and quantitative subjects.

Interpersonal skills: You must show that you can work with people and can sell.

Ambition: Investment banking is an all-consuming job. It requires you to abandon your social life. It is not a place for anyone who wants a family and quality time with friends.

Stamina: Eighty-hour work weeks are common in investment banking. You never know when you will be asked to fly across the country on a moment's notice and arrive ready to go to work. One newly arrived analyst worked nine months without a day off and claims he loved every minute of it.

The Right Personality: Each firm has its own personality, and yours should match it.

LAWYER

Lawyers interpret laws for the benefit of their clients—individuals or businesses.

Banks and financial services businesses, in particular, are governed by a multitude of federal and state laws and regulations. Corporate lawyers make sure that the companies they work for comply with these laws and regulations, and they represent the company when legal actions are brought. They review and prepare major contracts involving the corporation, negotiate with other lawyers, and review leases for the company's property.

As advocates, lawyers represent their companies in criminal and civil trials. As advisors, they provide advice about the company's legal rights and obligations and suggest courses of action.

Corporate lawyers often specialize in one area of law such as tax law, international law, civil rights law, securities law, or insurance law. Some act as trial lawyers and represent the company in court.

Corporate lawyers often work long hours, especially in the banking and finance areas where many documents must be filed for securities offerings, mergers, or divestitures.

Corporate lawyers handle most of the legal work required by the company, but time-consuming or highly technical matters may be given to outside law firms.

To practice law in a state, the lawyer must be licensed or admitted to the state's bar association. Most states require lawyers to pass a difficult exam, and many also require them to take a separate ethics examination.

Lawyers need a bachelor's degree. Undergraduate programs should emphasize communications, logic, public speaking, and general humanities courses. As with most jobs, familiarity with computers is helpful.

Lawyers are also required to complete at least three additional years of legal study and graduate from a law school approved by the American Bar Association. Many approved law schools offer night classes for people who must work full time.

Competition for law schools is vigorous, especially for the more prestigious schools. The first year and a half is spent studying basic law courses such as property law, procedures, and legal writing. The student then chooses a specialty such as tax law or corporate law and concentrates his or her study in that area.

Law firms often offer summer clerkships that provide opportunities to obtain references and jobs after graduation. Some specialties, such as tax, require the lawyer to obtain an advanced degree.

Few corporations have the resources to train new attorneys. They prefer to hire attorneys who have had experience in private law firms.

Once the lawyer is practicing, the studying does not end. It is critical that a lawyer stays abreast of what is happening in his or her client's industry and in the laws affecting that industry.

Beginning corporate lawyers earn an average of $37,000 a year, but that quickly reaches six figures and continues to grow as the lawyer's tenure with his or her company increases.

MARKETING

Marketing is matching products and services with buyers to make a profit for the company. It sounds like a much easier job than it is. Often, marketing, advertising, and public relations employees work together to sell the company's products or services.

Marketing people determine the demand for the company's services and products, identify potential customers, put together a pricing strategy to maximize market share and profits, monitor trends, identify new products and services, and oversee their development.

Sales professionals make sure that the products and services are sold and sales goals are met. They set up training programs to make sure salespeople understand what they are selling and how the products and services meet potential customers' needs. They determine the sales potential of new products and services and keep track of what customers want so that they can recommend new products or services or suggest that older ones be eliminated.

Advertising professionals usually represent the company with outside ad agencies. They decide what kind of advertising is needed and where that advertising will produce the best results. They are often directly involved in all creative aspects of a company's ads.

Public relations professionals use publicity to promote the company's products and services. They clarify or justify the company's decisions and points of view to make sure that the company's image is what it should be in the eyes of the public.

Marketing jobs usually require people to put in long hours, including evening and weekend work. Most professionals work under tight print or video production deadlines, and last-minute changes or problems are common. Many of the jobs require extensive traveling.

A bachelor's degree is necessary, and a liberal arts background is preferred. Most employees also need to take classes in accounting, marketing, economics, finance, and statistics, among others. Strong written and oral communications skills are a basic requirement.

The U.S. Department of Labor estimates that these jobs will grow faster than many other jobs through the end of the century because of increased competition for customers.

Annual salaries range from under $21,000 to more than $250,000, and many companies pay bonuses that can increase earnings by 10 percent or more.

RESEARCH ANALYST

Research analysts study securities—usually stocks—and make recommendations on what to buy and sell. Their advice is used by a wide range of other professionals in banking and finance, such as institutional and retail brokers, investment bankers, and trust and portfolio managers.

Analysts follow certain industries and companies within those industries, trying to learn everything they can about them. Most analysts are experts in twenty or thirty stocks in one or two industries. Some analysts may be experts in more than one hundred stocks.

Some of the things the analyst must learn about each company are its history, management, products, markets, financing, past earnings, and future earnings potential. To do this, they must understand accounting rules and study all kinds of financial reports and statements about the company.

Analysts take all the information they gather and write research reports, recommending buy, sell, or hold positions on every stock for which they are responsible. The analyst gives his or her recommendations to the company's brokers or, sometimes, directly to the company's customers.

Analysts have tremendous power in a brokerage firm. A good analyst whose recommendations result in profits for customers and the company becomes a hero. When a respected analyst changes his or her mind, the price of a stock can rise or fall based solely on the analyst's recommendation to buy or sell.

Analysts also spend time traveling, visiting the companies they follow and attending conventions and trade shows.

Once a year *Institutional Investor* magazine surveys institutional clients on who they think are the best analysts and publishes the results.

Top analysts can earn $500,000 a year. Starting salaries can be as high as $65,000 a year. Analysts also earn bonuses.

The Financial Analysts' Federation provides a designation of Chartered Financial Analyst to analysts who complete a series of rigorous essay examinations. To pass the exams, applicants need an extensive knowledge of accounting, economics, securities, and many other areas. But the CFA designation is almost as important as

77

an MBA, and in many firms it is the preferred designation for analysts.

SECRETARY (ADMINISTRATIVE ASSISTANT)

Behind every successful businessperson is a good secretary, sometimes also called an administrative assistant.

Secretaries keep their bosses functioning efficiently. They are the primary communicators of information as they perform a wide variety of important duties.

Secretaries make appointments for their bosses, answer callers' questions, maintain files, complete forms, take dictation, type correspondence and documents, schedule and coordinate meetings, make travel arrangements, and maintain information on personal computers, using spreadsheets, database management, and graphics programs.

Secretarial skills are in demand in almost every industry and profession. It is possible to move from one employer to another.

Employers want people who have at least a high school diploma and know basic office skills. Good time management and organizational skills are helpful.

Typing, spelling, and a good grasp of grammar and punctuation are musts to be a secretary. Shorthand or familiarity with dictation equipment is a plus, as is the ability to use word processing equipment and personal computers.

Good interpersonal skills are definitely an asset, since the secretary works closely with people at all levels both inside and outside the company.

Experienced secretaries can apply for the designation of Certified Professional Secretary (CPS) given by the Institute for Certifying Secretaries, a part of Professional Secretaries International. Candidates attain the designation by passing a series of examinations, and it is a mark of professional excellence.

Experienced secretaries can become executive secretaries to the partners or more senior members of a firm.

Secretaries must be able to adapt to change and learn how to use new equipment. As more and more office jobs are being automated, the secretary must develop a full range of skills in order to keep up with office technology. Many secretaries work for more than one person and must be willing and able to juggle sometimes conflicting assignments and priorities.

Annual salaries range from $19,100 to $38,400 a year and can go much higher for executive secretaries who work for senior executives.

TRADER

If you have seen pictures of the floor of an exchange such as the Pacific Stock Exchange, you have seen what bedlam looks like. People rushing around, shouting, waving hands and papers at each other. The action revolves around "pits," depressions in the floor where the traders buy and sell. It's hard to believe that all the frantic gestures and cryptic shouted messages mean something, but they do.

Traders buy and sell all kinds of things—securities, options, commodities—for their clients or firms. They match buyers and sellers, often using their own or their firm's money to close a deal. Fortunes are made and lost in seconds.

Traders have the fastest-paced jobs in banking and finance. As one experienced trader says, you have to master ". . . the essential trader's trick of doing at least four things at once, usually talking to a client on the phone while writing out a trading ticket and keeping a weather eye on the Dow-Jones tape and listening to the calls of other traders in the room."

Jobs on the floor are represented by the color of the jacket worn. Pages, runners, messengers, squads: light blue. Reporters: navy blue. Supervisors: green.

The people in street clothes are managers, directors, officers, and employees of other firms, such as:

- *Commission brokers*, who buy and sell securities for their firm's customers.
- Independent floor *brokers*, who are private entrepreneurs buying and selling for their own clients.
- Registered competitive *market makers*, who trade either for their own account or their firm's account when ordered to do so by an Exchange official. They accommodate all orders to keep the market moving or liquid.
- Competitive traders, who trade for their own accounts.
- Stock specialists who act as the focus of the market for specific stocks assigned to them.
- Agents who bring buyers and sellers together.

The major form of communication in the jumble is the famous Dow-Jones ticker tape. Once a strip of paper, it is now electronic. Each stock is identified by one, two, or three letters. Below and to the right of the symbol are the number of shares traded and the price.

News bulletins play across an electronic newsboard overlooking the pit.

Investment bankers trade thousands of shares of stock a day that represent millions of dollars. In some firms salespeople serve as middlepersons between the bank's customers and its traders who execute the

The floor of the Pacific Stock Exchange looks like a far different world than the sedate offices of bankers (courtesy Matrix).

transactions. In other firms the trader also acts as a salesperson.

Commercial bankers also maintain trading operations, mostly for the use of their institutional customers, but trading is dominated by the investment banks.

Traders cannot afford to leave the floor for a moment. They can lose millions of dollars by missing an opportunity to buy or sell a stock. There are no power lunches or even long bathroom breaks for traders during business hours: 9:30 to 4:00 Eastern Standard Time.

Traders must be able to think fast, concentrate in the midst of chaos, and make split-second decisions. These skills are more important than a degree. They also have to understand odds and risks and feel at ease with numbers.

Arbitrage is a form of trading. It involves simultaneously buying a contract in one market and selling it in another market for a price that is higher than the buying price. Profit is instantaneous. Arbitrage is becoming more and more common in mergers and acquisitions, when one company buys another company.

Business Week magazine described an arbitrageur in its August 13, 1984, issue: ". . . a trader who thrives on rumors, buying up shares quickly on hints of a raider's interest, in the hope of reselling them to anyone willing to pay a premium for control of a company." The movie *Wall Street* was the story of an arbitrageur, played by Michael Douglas.

One out of three traders burn out in a year. They can't take the stress or the pressure, or they can't make enough trades to earn an income.

Salaries start in the mid-twenties, but the average income for experienced traders reaches the six-figure range, usually within two years.

Interview: Allen Lee Dubbs,
Vice President and Specialist
Don C. Whitaker, Inc.
and
Arthur D. Penza
The Chicago Corporation
Members, Pacific Stock Exchange

Q. How did you get into this business?

A. *Penza*: I studied business management and economics in college and after graduating started working as a clerk on the options floor. I was a trading checker, did margin work, assisted a specialist.

I got a post four years ago and became a specialist myself, concentrating on a group of stocks and making a market. It's like being a traffic cop for the stocks.

Dubbs: I dropped out of college and was in data processing for ten years before starting as a clerk for a specialist on the Los Angeles floor. I clerked for four years, then I also became a specialist.

Q. Why did you choose this business?

A. *Dubbs*: I got an A in every math course I ever took. You have to be able to think in numbers.

Penza: And you have to think very fast, make quick decisions. When it's busy, you make lots of decisions based on what is going on in the world. Things can really move.

Dubbs: It's exciting and different every day.

Q. I've read that people burn out fast, that on the average traders are younger.

A. *Dubbs*: It can be intense. I take at least two months off each year.

Penza: When you start getting irritable and tense, you take a few days off.

Q. What are some of the benefits of the job?

A. *Dubbs*: There's no limit to the money you can

83

make. Your success or failure is measured by the money you make or lose. You immediately know how you're doing.

Penza: We get a report card every day. We also provide an important service: Our job is to keep a fair and orderly market.

Q. How do you handle it when you lose money?

A. *Dubbs*: You have to leave your work at work at the end of the day. But it's an intense business. You sometimes lie awake at night thinking about what happened.

You have to learn to put things in perspective and not beat yourself up. The gains have to outstrip the losses or you're not in this business very long.

Q. I understand from other research that a person doesn't need a formal education to be a trader. Rather, he or she needs a "trading feeling," a native intelligence. What else does it take?

A. *Dubbs*: It takes a certain personality, someone who can get along with others in close quarters in tense situations.

Penza: When you sit next to someone everyday, it's like having a spouse. Good communication skills help.

Dubbs: Some people try to get every penny they can out of a trade, and if they don't they yell and scream and slam things around.

Penza: People handle pressure differently.

Dubbs: You also have to think in numbers, be comfortable with numbers. It's all numbers. And we speak a different language here. A newcomer will say "4/8s" instead of "1/2." It takes a while to pick it up. You know within three months—or sooner—if someone is going to catch on.

Q. I keep hearing that if a person is interested in financial services he or she should read everything possible about the industry and how it works. What else should a young person do who is interested in becoming a trader?

Penza: Get a summer job with a large firm or an exchange. Get a feel for it.

Dubbs: Jump in and get your feet wet. There are so many different kinds of jobs, you have to check out the industry to find out what you think you might like.

TRUST OFFICER

The officers in a bank's trust department manage billions of dollars in assets for other people and organizations. Trust officers manage all kinds of assets, including real estate, securities, money, and even artwork. Some are also portfolio managers. These assets are placed in trust with the bank, which manages them according to the client's wishes.

Some of the trust accounts that a department may manage are money for wealthy people, endowments for schools, pension and profit-sharing money for companies, and retirement funds.

Sometimes a person makes arrangements to have the trust department manage his or her estate after death. This often happens if the person's heirs are minors.

The portfolio manager decides what securities should be bought for each portfolio he or she is responsible for. To do this, the portfolio manager relies on his or her own experience and on information gleaned from research analysts, each of whom follows one or more industries.

Portfolio managers are also responsible to an investment committee. All transactions must meet the requirements set down by the committee, which decides if certain investments are acceptable for its portfolios.

As in most areas of banking and finance, competition is fierce and getting fiercer. Trust and portfolio managers who earn the best returns on customers'

85

investments retain their existing clients and gain new ones through recommendations.

Some companies hire employees with BA degrees, but more and more companies require a graduate degree. Experience in other areas of securities or research analysis is usually required to be a portfolio manager, so it is not an entry-level job. More entry-level jobs are administrative assistant or portfolio assistant positions that allow employees to advance to more senior jobs.

Annual salaries range from the high teens for entry-level jobs to more than six figures for senior managers.

TYPIST AND WORD PROCESSOR

Typists and word processors type copies of handwritten, dictated, or already typed material. They type form letters, envelopes, manuals, original letters, reports, memos, technical documents, statistical tables, and large, complicated book-length materials.

Typists use a typewriter. Word processors use a computer or word processing equipment, which includes a keyboard, a video display terminal, and a printer. Many typists and word processors work in centralized locations, receiving material from a wide variety of departments throughout the organization. Others work in a specific area, supporting only that area's typing needs.

Many typists and word processors work part time, and some work at home if they have the equipment.

Typists and word processors need good typing, spelling, and grammar skills. Many employers want word processors to have formal training, since many different word processing software programs are available. These jobs are often entry-level jobs and offer the opportunity to move into higher-paying clerical, supervisory, or secretarial jobs.

Annual salaries average around $22,900 per year.

4

Insider Information

Employees in banking and finance often have access to information that is not available to the general public. It may be confidential information about a client or customer. Or employees may learn information about a company or customer before that information is released to the general public.

This kind of information is called insider information. If an employee reveals insider information to anyone, his or her career, along with the reputation of his or her bank or financial institution can be damaged. It is also against the law to use insider information for personal gain.

The following are some kinds of insider information to which employees in banking and finance have access:

- The sale or purchase of assets before the transactions are made public.
- Possible mergers and acquisitions.
- Accounting reports about a client or another company that are not available to the general public.
- Discussions of customer transactions.
- Letters or other documents that describe or mention deals.

For example, let's say you are working on the financial statements of XYX company because your client,

PQR company, wants to buy it. That is insider information. You cannot discuss what you know with anyone outside the company. You may not even be able to discuss it with some people inside the company. For instance, you could not tell a broker or trader about the pending acquisition. If you did and the broker or trader bought stock in XYX company, all involved would be breaking the law regarding using insider information for gain.

The key rule followed by all employees of banks and financial institutions is: Protect information.

Insider Trading: Not Worth the Risk

Trading that occurs because of inside information is called insider trading. This became a hot topic in the news in the 1980s, when several high-profile cases were exposed. Ivan Boesky became a household name in 1986 when he was arrested for insider trading and pled guilty to all charges. Boesky was fined $100 million, spent three years in prison, and was forever banned from trading on the New York Stock Exchange.

Insider trading did not cease to be a problem even after that well-publicized case. The Securities and Exchange Commission, which enforces insider trading regulations, reports that insider trading never really tapered off. In 1994 and 1995, the SEC investigated forty-five cases of insider trading. SEC officials say that the high number of mergers in the current economy accounts for much of the insider trading that occurs.

In an unusual case in 1996, the former chief financial officer of Intuit Inc. told his wife that the software company was going to be purchased by Microsoft. The wife shared the information with her son and daughter. Based on this information, the son, daughter, and three of their friends traded Intuit stock. The SEC filed a federal civil suit against the five who had traded as well as against the wife who passed on the information. All six settled the suit by paying $472,000, without admitting or denying wrongdoing.

The problem of insider trading has prompted stock markets to take steps to catch illegal traders. NASDAQ (National Association of Securities Dealers Automated Quotations) uses a computer system called SWAT, or Stock Watch Automatic Tracking, to monitor unusual trading.

5

Getting the Job You Want

Different jobs in banking and finance require different qualifications. A high school diploma will get you in the door for some jobs, such as broker or trader. Other entry-level positions that do not require a college degree are bank teller, bookkeeper, accounting clerk, data entry keyer, file clerk, secretary, and typist or word processor. For most of these jobs, you will need a thorough grounding in mathematics, an attention to detail, and a familiarity with computers. Be sure to take computer and math classes in high school, as well as accounting, bookkeeping, economics, and business classes if they are offered. If your school has a business club, you should consider joining.

If you are interested in being a broker or trader, you will also need a basic understanding of the way the stock market works.

As in most other fields, if you want to advance up the corporate ladder, you will eventually need a bachelor's degree. A bachelor's degree is also a minimum requirement for many of the entry-level jobs discussed in this book.

You need not study only business or accounting in college. Bankers and brokers come from all kinds of backgrounds—English literature, psychology, international relations, even art history. College undergraduates may want to concentrate on a major that shows they can think, analyze, and write. Many banks and financial companies prefer liberal arts majors who have strong communication and analytical skills and who like to work with people.

Most banks offer training programs that last about eighteen months, and it takes from four to eight years to reach the level of assistant vice president. Brokerages also offer their own training programs. Many of these programs send recruiters to college campuses in the spring to recruit graduating seniors.

Some of the higher-paying jobs in banking and finance demand a graduate or MBA degree, which means that you must make long-range plans if you want one of these positions. The superstar jobs on Wall Street, in banking, or anywhere else, require great qualifications and, in many cases, connections. You'll need high grades from the best schools for the really prestigious jobs, and you'll need to get plenty of work experience under your belt.

For all of these jobs, the job hunt begins right now.

Do Your Homework

To start planning for a job in this competitive field, do your research early.

Read books on investments and the companies involved in banking and finance. Some interesting ones are listed in the Appendix.

Read newspapers such as *The Wall Street Journal* and the *New York Times*. Read magazines such as *Forbes*, *Fortune*, and *Business Week* to gain an understanding of the industry. Consumer magazines such as *Money* and *Sylvia Porter's Personal Finance* will teach you how consumers view financial and banking services and products and teach you about the customers served by the financial services industry.

Watch television programs that discuss investments and the economy.

The Internet is also a good source of information. In addition to the home pages of individual companies, some online service providers offer web sites containing their own financial reports on many companies. So do some banks and financial service companies. Bank of America, for example, runs a free program for downloading economic research reports. Many banks and brokerages have their own home pages where you can learn more about the business. Online financial forums and discussion groups are other good places to find out about the worlds of banking and finance. You can also call companies directly and ask to be sent copies of their annual reports. If a company is publicly traded, you can also get a copy of the proxy report, which gives biographical and compensation information on the company's officers. Many companies will send you corporate histories or recruitment materials.

Even though you might not be actively seeking full-time employment until you graduate from college, you can still talk to on-campus recruiters to help you narrow your choice of jobs and companies. The college campus career center or placement office has information on the fields you are interested in. Learn as much as you can about the differences between jobs and companies.

Alumni from your college will probably be glad to talk with you and answer questions. But don't call on these people until you have done your homework: reading all you can on your own. Always send a cover letter explaining who you are, what you want, and that you will call in a week or two with your questions. This type of research is called an informational interview.

Informational Interviews
Prepare a list of questions beforehand so you will remember you want to cover. The more specific your

questions are, the better impression you will make and the more cooperation you will receive. The questions below should give you an idea of what to ask during an informational interview.

- How did you become interested in banking/finance?
- How did you get your first job?
- How should a person who is interested in banking or finance prepare for a career?
- What do you like most about your job?
- What do you like least about your job?
- What kind of challenges or problems do you have to deal with in your job?
- What sorts of skills do you need to succeed in your job?
- What is your typical day like?

Don't take more than thirty minutes of the person's time. At the end of each call, ask the person if he or she can recommend someone else for you to talk to. Send thank-you notes to everyone you interview.

Networking
Networking is one of the best ways to hear about potential jobs. Networking doesn't have to be an elaborate process. To start, make a list of all your friends. Then expand your network to include everyone else with whom you have even a passing acquaintance: relatives, your friends' parents, classmates, teachers, coaches, professors, religious leaders, counselors, local shopkeepers and businesspeople, your dentist and doctor, your family's lawyer, your parents' friends, the banker at your local branch, the people who gave you informational interviews, and anyone else you know.

Write each person's name down on a separate index card or make space for them in a computer file. Then begin contacting everyone in your network. Ask them specific questions: Do they know of any jobs that you might be interested in? How about at their company? Can they introduce you to someone who might give you more information? As in the informational interviews, don't forget to thank them afterward. Keep track of when you speak to each person and what they told you. A simple way is to write it directly on the index card or add it to the computer file. These steps help you build a network that will prove valuable not only when you are ready for full-time employment, but when you want a summer job at one of the firms you are interested in.

Internships

Internships are very valuable. Part-time and summer jobs provide experience-based learning. You have a chance to "reality test" how you feel or fit in a specific job situation. You get first-hand experience and the ability to see how your education fits into the real world. You also develop a track record of competence, getting things done, building self-confidence, and garnering recommendations for future employers.

To prepare for an internship, work with someone on the college career placement staff to explore areas of interest, kinds of activities, relationships, roles, and what excites you.

Preparing a Résumé

Now that you've researched possible banking careers and know which kind of job interests you most, it's time to put that knowledge to good use. The first step in landing an interview is crafting the perfect résumé.

A résumé is basically an outline of what you've done

and where you want to go. Think of it as a sophisticated sales tool, designed to sell the thing you know best: yourself. If you have never done one before, take some time to sit down and think about what you would like to say about yourself. Feel free to draw up several different drafts and experiment with the best way to package your skills. Whatever you choose to say about yourself, you should include the following information on your résumé:

- Your name, address, and telephone number.
- Education. Include where you went to high school or college, your grade point average, what degrees you received and when, and any academic honors you won. If you are attending or have graduated from college, it is not necessary to include your high school history.
- Work experience. List the names and locations (city and state) of companies that you have worked for and a short list of your responsibilities at each job. This can include part-time or temporary work, internships, and any volunteer work that you have done (although some people choose to include volunteer work in a separate category).
- Membership in clubs or organizations. Mention any varsity or intramural sports, especially if you were captain or team leader, as well as participation in other activities.
- Military history, if applicable.
- Skills. Be sure to list any computer, communication, and foreign language skills you have. Show proof that you can write, analyze, and think on your feet.

You can also include the following if you wish:

- Career objective. This is the name of the job that you are applying for, such as assistant branch manager or junior accountant.
- Relevant high school or college courses you have taken.
- Personal data: birth date and marital status, hobbies, other interests.

Most people who are in the early stages of their career organize their skills and experiences in a chronological format. To follow this format, list your experience beginning with your most recent job first and work your way backward. This sample résumé was written in a chronological format. People with many years of work experience sometimes list their employment history in a functional rather than a chronological format. This means that they group their jobs and related experience under different categories, such as supervisory experience, manual labor experience, or customer service experience.

SAMPLE RÉSUMÉ

Jenny McGrath
143 Valencia Street
San Francisco, CA 94116
(415) 555-8396

Education

San Francisco State University, San Francisco, CA
Bachelor of Arts expected May 1998
Major: Economics. Minor: Russian Literature.
GPA: 3.45

Work Experience	*Bank Teller,* Wells Fargo Bank, San Francisco, CA June 1996–present
	Process withdrawals and deposits; wire money; issue traveler's checks, foreign currency, savings bonds, and certificates of deposit; balance cash against transactions. Won the Employee of the Year Award for the San Bruno Avenue Branch in 1997.
	Volunteer Team Leader, University Outreach Project September 1995-present
	Supervise ten overnight camping trips a year for groups of inner-city girls ages 8–14.
	Waitress, The Lobster Pot, Half Moon Bay, CA June 1995–August 1995
	Served an average of fifty customers a night in a fine-dining atmosphere.
Skills	Excellent math, writing, and customer service skills. Can operate Microsoft Word and WordPerfect word-processing software. Fluent in Russian and Spanish.

References available upon request.

What can you put in your résumé that will especially impress an interviewer who has seen and heard it all?

- A knowledge of accounting. You don't have to major in it—and you probably shouldn't unless you want to be an accountant—but you need a working knowledge of accounting principles. It also shows that you are serious about your intent to pursue a job in banking or finance.
- Work experience in finance or banking. Choose summer jobs in the banking or financial services industry. Most branch offices of brokerage firms use college summer help. Some offer paid and unpaid internships. Listing one or more of these jobs will give you an advantage. Many banks hire college students as part-time tellers, clerical employees, and data entry operators.
- Work experience in sales. If you can't land a job in the finance or banking areas, sell something. Many of the jobs in banking and finance require sales experience.
- Memberships. Companies want both leaders and team players. Make sure your résumé shows that you are one or the other (or both).
- Relevant courses. Try to take courses in economics, math, English composition, finance, debate, and computer science. These courses are especially important if you major in a non-business subject such as history, English, or psychology.

When preparing your résumé, keep these tips in mind:

- Keep it short and to the point. Use the fewest words possible to say what you want to say. Your résumé should fit on one page; use two pages only if absolutely necessary.
- Make it easy to read. Organize the different sec-

tions so that key points grab the reader's attention. It's okay to use italics and bold type for emphasis, but use them sparingly.

- Be dynamic. Use action words whenever possible: directed, analyzed, initiated, launched, etc.
- Proofread your résumé until you know that it is perfect. Any typos or grammatical errors could cost you an interview. To be absolutely sure it is perfect, have someone else proof it too.
- Use a standard typeface and print the résumé on white, cream, or ivory paper. Do not skimp on the quality of paper. Remember that this will be the employer's first impression of you. Make it a good one!

Cover Letters

A cover letter should accompany your résumé. It should emphasize why you are particularly qualified for the job. Cover letters are short, just a few paragraphs at most. The first paragraph usually includes the title of the job you are applying for and the place that you saw the job opening or the person who told you about it. Cover letters are a good place to put all that research you did earlier to good use. Feel free to mention any facts that you dug up about the company: if the company had record profits, experienced a recent merger, or prides itself on a particular kind of service or product. Make sure to print your cover letter on the same kind of paper as your résumé. Also carefully proof the letter before you send it out. Have someone else proof it too.

SAMPLE COVER LETTER

143 Valencia Street
San Francisco, CA 94116
April 28, 1998

Mr. Fred Nagasaki
Vice President
United Savings Bank
San Francisco, CA 94313

Dear Mr. Nagasaki:

I am writing to you to apply for the position of personal trust assistant that was advertised in the *San Francisco Chronicle* on April 27. My résumé is enclosed for your review.

I am currently finishing my senior year at San Francisco State University. My major courses have included Micro and Macro Economic Theory, International Business, and Computer Based Information Systems. I also have a minor in Russian Literature.

For the past two years, I have worked part-time during the school year and full-time during summers as a bank teller for Wells Fargo. In this time I have gained a thorough grounding in basic bank procedures and services. Additionally, I have become skilled at dealing with all types of customers and meeting their special needs as quickly and efficiently as possible.

I believe that I have what it takes to make an excellent assistant in the field of personal trust. My background in banking, combined with my knowledge of the field of economics, would be an asset to your trust department at Union Savings Bank. I would welcome a chance to meet with you and discuss your requirements for the position in person.

I look forward to hearing from you.
Sincerely,

Jenny McGrath
(415) 555-8396

References

In addition to your résumé, you should also have a list of at least three people who know you fairly well and who have agreed to provide a reference for you. These can be former employers, high school teachers, college professors, or anyone except relatives. Although you will not be listing them on your résumé, you can expect to be asked for this list of references during an interview. Print the list of references on the same kind of paper that your résumé is printed on. Ask people if you can use them for a reference *before* giving their names to a prospective employer. Make sure that the people you choose have a positive view of you and will give you an excellent reference. For each reference, list the person's name, job title, company name and address, and telephone number.

The Interview

You've sent out your résumés and cover letters. Now companies are beginning to contact you for interviews. Don't panic! Think of the interview as a fact-finding mission, not a test. It's up to you to figure out if you would be comfortable working at the company. So go ahead and ask questions of your own. What are the possibilities for career advancement? What would your typical day be like? Why did the interviewer choose to work for that particular company? What are appropriate goals for the person in the job in question to set?

Spend some time before the interview thinking of questions that you might be asked and the answers you would give. On the day of the interview, dress conservatively. Bankers dress to blend in, not to stand out, so wear a conservative business suit to your interview. Bring along an extra copy or two of your résumé and your cover letter.

Relax, and try to remain positive. Eventually, you will get a job. And then the real work begins!

Interview: Susan Garcia, Assistant Vice President
Employment Office–North
Bank of America
and
Elaine Sczuka, Assistant Vice President
Placement Services
Wells Fargo Bank
and
Stephanie McAuliffe, Vice President
Central Training and Development
Wells Fargo Bank

Q. Does a young person need a college degree for a career in banking?

A. *Garcia*: It depends on what you want to do. You don't need a degree to work in operations as a first-line supervisor or manager if you have the aptitude. For general supervisory jobs, you need people skills and on-the-job knowledge.

A college degree is an entrée to management training programs for lending, operations, recruitment. It gives you an edge.

Some jobs require an MBA, such as the higher-level credit jobs where you are lending to large companies, or you would need a CPA for a job in finance.

Generally, the higher the goal, the higher the degree you need.

Sczuka: Most lenders have MBA degrees. You need the sophistication an MBA gives you when you are dealing with a *Fortune* 500 CEO.

Sales skills are also very valuable.

Q. What should a person study in college?

A. *Garcia*: I believe you should study either business or liberal arts. If you want to concentrate on retail banking, you should study economics or finance.

McAuliffe: It's hard to generalize. Every corporate culture is different.

Q. How valuable is it to work for a bank part time before making a full-time commitment?

A. *Sczuka*: Banks are built around part-time jobs. A large number of college students are working and going to school at the same time.

Garcia: It's an excellent way to get the feel of the business. There really is a gap between school and the job. Working while you learn brings it all together.

When you work as a teller or in the back-room support functions, you obtain information about the business that you can't get outside the bank. It also makes you what we call an internal candidate: You are a known quantity to your manager, who can recommend you for training programs.

McAuliffe: Wells Fargo has 24-hour phone customer service. It's not necessarily a career track, but it provides flexible working hours.

You can walk into a branch and get a job, but once you are on board, maximize your opportunities to learn about the company. Read the brochures the company produces. Ask questions. The more you get into it, the more you get out of it.

Q. I've read a lot about change and the need to adapt to a changing environment. How true is that?

A. *McAuliffe*: Change is so rapid that there are no longer traditional career paths. In the early 1970s, you had true career paths. You moved from job to job in a fairly orderly way. That's no longer true. In five years the job you do could become very different, or even obsolete. An operations manager position could become a sales job that requires different skills. That is especially true for branch jobs. You need the broadest array of skills possible, especially sales experience.

Sczuka: You need a good sales record because banking is so sales-oriented now. For instance, the personal banking officers at Wells Fargo sell products to customers. They have to identify customer needs and sell them the bank's products that meet those needs.

Garcia: You have to be very flexible. You have to be able to work in a number of different markets and may even be willing to relocate.

You may have to accept sideways steps if they give you a chance to broaden your knowledge and make you more of an asset to the company. Moving up isn't always best. You have to look at the broader picture.

I'm a good example of how that works. I worked full time for Bank of America and went to school at night. I moved up from a clerical job to a supervisory one. When I finished my degree, I went into Communications, then became a supervisor, manager, and now I'm head of Employment-North. Many of my moves were sideways moves.

Q. What are the hot jobs in banking right now?

A. *Garcia*: Investment banking. Commercial banking. Private banking.

Sczuka: Lending is very big.

Q. What does an employment interviewer look for during interviews?

A. *Garcia*: You want to see interest in the company, what people know about the company, and why they have chosen your company over others. You want to know their short- and long-time goals and how they will

104

fit into the organization. Whether they work best in an entrepreneurial environment or are better as team players.

Sczuka: Practice presenting yourself professionally.

Q. What can a high school student do now to prepare for a job in banking?

A. *McAuliffe*: Get a summer job at a bank. Read the business page of the newspaper and develop an awareness of what the business involves. Comparison-shop checking accounts, not only to make sure you get a good deal, but to understand something about banking and competition. You can learn a lot about a company just by being an informed consumer.

Sczuka: Do your homework. Do informational interviews. Talk to employees at your local bank branch.

Stick with it. People are often busy when you call for information. Try again until you get through to them.

McAuliffe: Some community agencies set up mentorships or sponsor a day on the job. Find out what's available in the banking area and take advantage of it.

This is a people-intensive business that needs bright, intelligent people.

Glossary

accountant   Specialist who prepares and analyzes the financial transcactions of a business and may make recommendations for financial decisions.

accounting   Keeping track of financial records: how money flows into, through, and out of a business.

administration   Department of a company that provides support services, such as equipment requisition and personnel management.

American Stock Exchange (Amex)   Exchange where stocks of lesser-known companies are bought and sold.

analyst   Specialist in a particular industry or several industries. The analyst researches everything available about his or her specialty, synthesizes that information, and makes recommendations about what stocks within that industry a company should buy and sell. Good analysts can forecast future industry trends.

annual report   Statement of how a company has done financially in the past year.

appraiser   Person who estimates the value of real estate or personal property.

arbitrage   Taking advantage of price differences in securities or commodities traded on different exchanges, or between new and old securities of a single company. The arbitrageur takes opposing positions in the hope of turning a profit from temporary price differences.

assets   Property owned by or owed to a company or person.

auditor Person who examines financial records to ensure their accuracy.

automated teller machine (ATM) Electronic banking machine that takes deposits and issues withdrawals.

average Measure of trends in stock prices.

bank Company that offers financial services to individuals and institutions.

banker Person who works in the banking industry.

bank operations Functions that support daily banking activities; also called back-room operations.

bear market Period during which stock prices go down.

benefit managers Professionals who design and administer benefits programs.

benefits Nonmonetary compensation given to employees, such as health care, life insurance, and retirement plans.

bond Debt security. A company issues bonds to people and organizations that lend the company money. The company pays either a set or a fluctuating rate of interest to the bondholders and promises to redeem the bonds at a future date.

bookkeeper Person who maintains financial ledgers.

broker Agent who buys and sells securities for customers.

brokerage Company that offers financial and investment services to individual and institutional customers.

budget Written plan for handling income and expenditures.

bull market Period during which stock prices go up.

Business Administration Study of how businesses are operated, of business principles and practices.

call Option to buy a security.

capital Goods or money used to generate income.

capital market Security market such as the bond or stock market.

cash flow Movement of money into, through, and out of an organization.

cash manager Controller of the flow of money.

Certificate in Management Accounting (CMA) Designation conferred by the National Association of Accountants (NAA) to those who pass a series of exams and meet certain standards.

Certificate of Accreditation in Taxation Designation conferred by the Accreditation of Council for Accountancy of the National Society of Public Accountants.

certificate of deposit Savings instrument deposited for a specified period of time.

Certified Information Systems Auditor (CISA) Designation conferred by the EDP Auditors Association on candidates who complete five years of experience in the field.

Certified Internal Auditor (CIA) Designation conferred by the Institute of Internal Auditors, Inc., on graduates of colleges and universities who have two years of experience in the area and who pass a four-part exam.

Certified Professional Secretary Designation given by the Institute for Certifying Secretaries, a part of Professional Secretaries International. Candidates must pass a series of exams to obtain the designation.

Certified Public Accountant (CPA) Licensed and regulated accountant.

Chartered Financial Analyst Designation conferred by the Financial Analysts Federation on research analysts who complete a series of exams.

check Authorization for a bank to draw money from an account and pay it to the person or organization to whom the check was written.

checking account On-demand deposit that can be withdrawn by checks.

clearing agent Agency that provides capital and office support and functions as a bank for traders.

clerk Employee who keeps track of records and files and handles various pieces of office equipment, such as typewriters, calculators, and computers.

cold call Call to a stranger by phone or in person to try to sell him or her something.

collateral Something of value put up to secure a loan.

commercial bank Bank that provides services to corporations and individuals.

commission Fee earned or amount charged for buying and selling something, such as stocks.

commodities Objects of commerce, such as crops, hogs, lumber, and gold, that are bought and sold.

Commodity Futures Trading Commission (CFTC) Federal agency that regulates commodity trading.

community bank Small, usually suburban or rural, bank.

compensation Salary and monetary rewards, such as bonuses, given to employees.

compensation manager Executive who develops pay policies for a company.

compliance Actions of a company to meet government regulations and its own corporate standards.

computer operator Person who handles data by computer.

computer programmer Person who writes computer instructions in a computer language.

conglomerate   Corporation made up of many different parts or companies.

controller   Financial manager responsible for the accounting, audit, and budget departments of a company.

corporate money manager   Specialist who manages a corporation's money, recommending and managing its investments.

corporate securities   Stocks or bonds issued by a company to raise money.

credit   Time given for payment for purchases.

credit union   Cooperative association that offers banking services such as savings accounts and loans to its members.

customer service representative   Employee who deals directly with customers, resolves customer problems, and makes sure that the customer receives good service.

data processing   Function that inputs and works with information on computers.

dealer   Person who acts as a principal. Dealers buy securities for their own accounts and then sell them to customers.

depositor   Person who puts money in a bank account.

deposit   Money or valuables placed in a bank for safekeeping.

deposit slip   Paper record of money placed in a bank account.

deregulation   Removal of government regulations from an industry.

discount brokerage   Company that offers financial and investment services at reduced commission fees.

dividend   Earnings on stocks; money or additional shares of stock paid to stockholders based on number of shares owned.

Dow-Jones average   Average of the prices of thirty outstanding industrial stocks listed on the NYSE.

Dow-Jones ticker tape   Electronic record of buys and sells of securities.

economics   Science of the production, distribution, and consumption of goods and services.

economist   Person who studies and applies the principles of economics.

electronic banking   Banking services provided by computer.

employee benefit plans   Insurance and savings plans offered by companies to employees and their families, such as life insurance, retirement plans, health care, vacations, and profit-sharing.

Equal Employment Opportunity (EEO)   Hiring of people without regard to factors unrelated to the job, such as race, sex, or sexual preference.

equity   Stock that represents ownership in a company.

Federal Reserve System   Agency established in 1913 by the Federal Reserve Act to regulate banking.

finance   Science of managing money.

financial statements   Various presentations of a company's financial status that appear in its annual report.

foreign currency   Money issued by foreign governments.

floor   Trading area of an exchange.

futures contract   Agreement to buy or sell a commodity at a future date.

Garn-St. Germain Depository Institutions Act: Legislation passed in 1982 that allowed banks to offer new products and deregulated much of the industry.

Glass-Steagall Act   Legislation passed in 1933 that separated commercial banks and investment banks

111

and prohibited commercial banks from underwriting corporate securities.

government bonds Debt obligation issued by federal, state, or municipal government.

grievance Complaint by a union employee against the company.

holding company Nonoperating company that owns or has a controlling interest in the securities of other companies that do operate as businesses. For instance, Bank America Corporation is the holding company for Bank of America and Seafirst Corporation among other companies. Seafirst Corporation, in turn, is a holding company for Seafirst Bank.

home banking System that allows customers to make banking transactions with personal computers in their offices or homes.

home improvement loan Loan made to upgrade a home using the home as collateral.

Human Resources Department of a company that establishes personnel policies and procedures.

individual retirement account Savings instrument that defers and reduces taxes on deposits.

inflation Rise in prices and wages.

insiders Directors, officers, and major securities holders of a corporation; usually they own more than 10 percent of the company.

insider trading Buying or selling securities on the basis of infomation that has not been made public; a violation of federal law.

institution Financial company that invests large amounts of money, such as an insurance company, a corporate pension fund, a mutual fund, or a trust department. Most of the money traded in the various securities markets comes from institutions.

institutional broker Middle person between institutional investors and research analysts.

institutional investor Organization having large amounts of money invested in securities.

insurance company Business that sells protection against certain losses to individuals or corporations.

insured savings vehicle Savings investment guaranteed by the government.

interest-bearing checking account Checking account that pays interest on deposits.

interest rate Amount of money paid to depositors or investors on their money or to lenders; usually a percentage of the principal.

internal auditor Employee who audits a company's financial transactions and procedures.

investment bank Bank that underwrites securities; it helps clients raise money through mergers and acquisitions, acting as a middleman between companies and investors.

investor Person who commits money to an investment in the hope of earning more money.

job analyst Person who compiles information on job duties.

license Permission by authority to perform certain activities such as selling securities.

load Sales charge imposed on investors in mutual funds.

loan Money borrowed.

loan officer Bank employee who makes decisions about lending money to customers.

management fee Fee charged to investors by mutual funds for professional management.

margin Customer's equity in securities purchased on credit from a broker.

marketing Matching products and services to customers to make a profit for the company.

market makers Traders who trade for their own accounts or for their firm's account when an Exchange official orders them to do so.

McFadden Act Legislation passed in 1927 that forbade banks to open branches outside their home state.

merger Combination of two or more companies into one.

merger and acquisition Takeover of one company by another.

microfilm Documents maintained on film, not paper.

money market account High-quality, short-term instrument such as certificate of deposit, treasury bill, and commerical paper.

money market mutual fund Pool of investors' money used to buy money market securities.

money market securities Short-term obligations of borrowers such as the U.S. Treasury, federal, state and local governments, banks, and corporations. Usually the least risky types of investments.

mortgage Use of a home as collateral on a loan to pay for the home.

municipal bond Debt obligation to raise money; issued by a city, town, village, or state.

mutual fund Pool of investors' money used to buy investments in larger amounts than would be possible for individual investors. The money is invested in a diversified list of securities chosen by the fund manager.

mutual savings bank Nonprofit business owned by its depositors.

National Association of Securities Dealers (NASD) Association of brokers and dealers in the over-the-counter market.

New York Stock Exchange (NYSE) The world's largest securities exchange, located at 11 Wall Street, with a trading floor the size of a football field. More than 2,000 stocks are listed on the so-called Big Board and are traded on the floor of the exchange daily.

NYSE index Average of all the stocks listed on the NYSE.

option Right to buy or sell a stock at a fixed price by a certain date.

over-the-counter market (OTC) Trading of securities not listed on any exchange; OTC traders buy and sell stocks and bonds via computer.

Personnel Department Department of a company that handles human resources functions such as staffing, equal employment opportunity, training, compensation, and benefits.

pit Locations on the trading floor where commodities brokers and traders work.

portfolio Collection of securities held by an individual or institutional investor.

premium Price paid for an option.

printout Hard copy of computer data.

private bank Bank owned by private investors and offering limited services to a small group of wealthy investors.

private placement Securities transaction between two or more private parties without involvement of an exchange.

privileged information Confidential information communicated between two parties.

prospectus Document filed with the Securities and Exchange Commission when a company offers stock for sale.

publicly traded Bought or sold on an exchange.

115

public relations Use of ads and publicity to inform customers of the products and services the company has to offer.

put Option to sell a security.

recession Slowdown of the economy.

recruiter Employee who locates and hires qualified people for open positions.

registered representative Broker or account executive who has passed certain tests and met standards set by the NYSE, the NASD, or both.

research analyst *See* analyst.

retail bank Bank providing services to individuals.

retail broker Broker who advises individual investors on what investments to make to meet their goals.

retailer Business that sells goods to consumers for personal or household use.

retirement planning Planning for investments to provide a certain level of income at retirement.

safe deposit box Container placed in a bank safe for the storage of valuables.

sales manager Executive who supervises the sale of a company's products and services.

savings account Vehicle for investing money and receiving regular guaranteed interest payments.

savings and loan association Institution owned by depositors or stockholders that chiefly provides mortgages.

seat Membership on a stock exchange with the right to buy and sell securities on that exchange.

securities Stocks and bonds.

Securities and Exchange Commission (SEC) Federal agency established to regulate trading in securities.

selling group Group of investment banks and brokerages that agree to sell securities.

spread   Difference between two prices; for instance, the difference between what an investment bank pays for an issue of stock and what it sells the stock for.

Standard & Poors   Indexes of 425 industrial stocks and 500 other stocks traded on the NYSE.

stock   Share of ownership in a company.

stockbroker   Person who buys and sells stock for individual investors.

stock exchange   Place where a market for securities is made.

stockholder   Person who owns shares of stock and has the right to vote on the election of the company's directors and other affairs.

syndicate   Group of banks that agree to underwrite securities.

tax   Money levied by a government authority on income, profits, property, etc.

tax shelter   Investment having tax benefits.

time certificate of deposit   Investment of a specific amount of money for a given period of time in order to earn a higher rate of interest.

trader   Person who buys and sells stocks for profit, taking advantage of small price changes.

Trust Department   Department of a bank that manages assets for individuals or institutions.

trust fund   Investments held by one party, such as a bank, for the benefit of another party, such as a child.

underwriting   Assuming the risk of insurance or agreeing to purchase an issue of a security for the purpose of selling it to the public.

wholesale banking   Commercial banking.

withdrawal   Taking money out of an account.

Appendix

American Bankers Association (ABA)
1120 Connecticut Avenue NW
Washington, DC 20036
(202) 663-5000
Web site: http://www.aba.com

American Institute of Banking (AIB)
1120 Connecticut Avenue NW
Washington, DC 20036
(202) 663-5429

American Financial Services Association
919 18th Street NW
Washington, DC 20006
(202) 296-5544
Web site: http://www.americanfinsvcs.com

American Institute of Certified Public Accountants
1121 Avenue of the Americas
New York, NY 10036-8775
(212) 596-6200
Web site: http://www.aicpa.com

American Stock Exchange
86 Trinity Place
New York, NY 10006
(212) 306-1000
Web site: http://www.amex.com

Bank Administration Institute
1 North Franklin Street, Suite 1000
Chicago, IL 60606
(312) 553-4600
Web site: http://www.bai.org

Commodity Exchange
4 World Trade Center
New York, NY 10048
(212) 938-2000

Credit Union Executives Society
6410 Enterprise Lane
Madison, WI 53719-1143
(608) 271-2664
e-mail: cues@cues.org
Web site: http://www.cues.org

Financial Women International
200 North Glebe Road, Suite 1430
Arlington, VA 22203-3728
(703) 807-2007
e-mail: fwistaff@erols.com
Web site: http://www.fwi.org

Institute of Financial Education
111 East Wacker Drive
Chicago, IL 60601-4680
(312) 364-0010
Web site: http://www.ifegotheinstitute.com

Institute of Internal Auditors
249 Maitland Avenue
Altamonte Springs, FL 32701-4201
Web site: http://www.theiia.org

Institute of Management Accountants
10 Paragon Drive
Montvale, NJ 07645
(800) 638-4427
Web site: http://www.imanet.org

New York Stock Exhcange
11 Wall Street
New York, NY 10005
(212) 656-3000
Web site: http://www.nyse.com

For Further Reading

Aliber, Robert Z. *The International Money Game.* New York: Basic Books, 1987.

Allison, Eric W. *The Raiders of Wall Street.* New York: Lanham Madison, 1986.

American Banker Bond Buyer Staff. *Rand McNally Bankers Directory*, 2d ed. 3 vols. Chicago: Rand McNally & Co., 1990.

Bloch, Ernest. *Inside Investment Banking.* Burr Ridge, IL: Irwin Professional Publishing, 1988.

Eaton, Bruce. *No Experience Necessary: Make $100,000 a Year as a Stockbroker.* New York: Simon & Schuster, 1987.

Lewis, Michael. *Liar's Poker: Rising Through the Wreckage on Wall Street.* New York: Viking Penguin, 1990.

Little, Jeffrey B., and Lucien Rhodes. *Understanding Wall Street*, 14th ed. New York: McGraw-Hill, 1997.

Maturi, Richard J. *Wall Street Words: From Annuities to Zero Coupon Bonds*, rev. ed. Burr Ridge, IL: Irwin Professional Publishing, 1995.

Morgan, Bradley. *Business and Finance Career Directory.* Detroit: Visible Ink Press, 1993.

Morris, Kenneth, and Alan M. Siegel. *The Wall Street Journal Guide to Understanding Money and Investing.* New York: Simon & Schuster, 1994.

Ring, Trudy. *Careers in Finance.* Lincolnwood, IL: VGM Career Horizons, 1993.

Simpson, Carolyn. *Choosing a Career in Banking and Finance.* New York: Rosen Publishing Group, 1997.

Tamarkin, Bob. *The New Gatsbys: Fortunes and Misfortunes of Commodity Traders*. New York: William Morrow, 1985.

Woelfel, Charles, J. *Encyclopedia of Banking and Finance*, 10th ed. Burr Ridge, IL: Irwin Professional Publishing, 1996.

Index

A

accountant
  and computer software, 27
  certifications, 27-28
  duties of, 26
  earnings, 28
  qualifications needed, 27, 28
America Online, 23
appraiser
  certifications, 46
  duties of, 45-46
arbitrage, 82
ATM, 1

B

bank mergers, 14
bank teller
  duties of, 29, 33
  earnings, 33
  qualifications, 29, 33
  training, 33
banking
  as a career
    cover letters, 99-101
    general preparation for, 91-92
    general qualifications for, 90-91, 98
    informational interviews, 92-93
    internships, 94
    interviewing, 101-102
    networking, 93-94
    preparing a resume, 94-99
    references, 101
    training programs in, 91
  broad areas of

bank administration and
  accounting, 16
community banking, 17
consumer banking (a.k.a.
  retail banking), 15-16
operations/data processing,
  16
public relations and
  marketing, 16-17
trust banking, 16
changes in, 4-5
commercial, 8, 16
effect of customer demands on,
  5, 9
future of, 11-13
  advantages of new
    technology, 13
  debit cards, 12-13
  disadvantages of new
    technology, 13
  electronic banking, 12
  smart cards, 11-12
  super-ATMs, 11
investment
  definition of, 8
new products and services in,
  10
  discount brokerage, 10
  foreign exchange trading, 10
  home banking, 10
bonds, 67
bookkeeper/accounting clerk
  duties of, 34
  earnings, 34
  qualifications, 34
brokers
  building business, 37-38

certifications, 35
duties of, 35
earnings, 37, 38
qualifications, 38, 41
training, 37
types of, 35

C
capital, 67
Certified Financial Planner
(CFA), 61
Certified Public Accountants
(CPAs), 27, 28
Chicago Board of Trade, 47
clerical supervisor and manager
duties of, 42-43
earnings, 43
qualifications, 43
work hours, 43
College for Financial Planning,
57, 58, 60-61
commercial banker
duties of, 43-44
earnings, 45
qualifications, 45
training, 44-45
commodities
definition of, 47
exchanges, 48
futures, 47
options, 47
trading, 47-48
commodity trader
earnings, 49
training, 48-49
competition
among banks, 14, 44
between banks and nonbank
financial services firms, 2,
5, 9, 22, 69
between discount and full-
service brokerages, 38
computer operators
duties of, 50-51
earnings, 51
qualifications, 51

training, 51
work hours, 51
computers
effect on financial services
industry, 27, 38, 49, 66

D
data entry keyer
duties of, 51-52
earnings, 52
qualifications, 52
deregulation, 2, 5, 8-10, 22
discount online brokerages, 23

E
economist
duties of, 52-53
earnings, 53
job opportunities, 53
qualifications, 53
Equal Employment Opportunity
(EEO), 64

F
file clerk
duties of, 53, 55
earnings, 55
qualifications, 55
training, 55
financial manager
duties of, 55-56
earnings, 57
job opportunities, 56
other titles for, 55, 56
qualifications, 55, 56
financial planner
certifications, 58
duties of, 57, 59-60
earnings, 60
job opportunities, 58
qualifications, 58, 61, 63-64
why consulted by clients, 59
foreign language
as a qualification for a banking
career, 15

G
Garn-St. Germain Depository
    Institutions Act, 9
generalist, 17, 18
Glass-Steagall Act, 8, 68

H
historical roles of banks and
    brokerages, 1-2, 4, 5-6
human resources professionals
    duties of, 64-65
    earnings, 65
    qualifications, 65
    types of, 64-65

I
insider information
    and the law, 87, 88
    defined, 87
insider trading, 70-71, 88-89
institutional broker
    duties of, 65-66
    earnings, 66
    qualifications, 66
interest, 8, 9
internet, 23, 92
international banking, 14
interstate banking, 14
investment banker
    duties of, 67-68, 69
    earnings, 70, 71, 72
    qualifications, 71, 72-73
    training, 71
    work hours, 70, 72, 73
investment banking
    analyst programs in, 71-72
    as a team activity, 68
    intense competition in, 67, 69-
        70

L
lawyer
    duties of, 73-74
    earnings, 75
    qualifications, 74
    training, 74-75

    types of, 74
    work hours, 74

M
marketing, 75
marketing bank services,
    importance of, 10
marketing professionals
    earnings, 76
    job outlook, 76
    qualifications, 76
    types of, 75-76
    work hours, 76
MBA degree
    and salary, 72
    needed in international
        banking, 15
    needed in investment banking,
        72
    number of women earning an,
        24
    when needed, 18, 27, 91
McFadden Act of 1927, 14
money market mutual funds, 9

N
NASDAQ (National Association
    of Securities Dealers
    Automated Quotations), 89
National Bank Acts of 1863 and
    1864, 6
New York Stock Exchange, 21, 35

R
research analyst
    certifications, 77-78
    duties of, 76-77
    earnings, 77
    qualifications, 77

S
secretary
    certifications, 78-79
    duties of, 78
    earnings, 79
    job opportunities, 79

qualifications, 78, 79
Securities and Exchange
     Commission, 26, 88
separation of commercial and
     investment banking, 8
sex discrimination, 24
"spread," 8, 9, 48, 69

T
trader
  and burnout, 82, 83
  benefits of being a, 83-84
  duties of, 79, 80, 82
  earnings, 82
  qualifications, 82
  types of, 80
  work hours, 82
trust officer
  and competition, 85-86
  duties, 85
  earnings, 96
  qualifications, 86
trustworthy paper currency, 6
typist/word processor
  duties, 86
  earnings, 86
  job opportunities, 86
  qualifications, 86
  work hours, 86

W
Wall Street
  and scandals, 20
  and technology, 22-23
  and women, 23-25
  as heart of financial services
    industry, 22
  history of, 21
  jobs on, 20-21
  location, 21
  perceptions of, 19-20